what do we know and what should we do about...?

immigration

Jonathan Portes

Los Angeles | London | New Delhi
Singapore | Washington DC | Melbourne

Los Angeles | London | New Delhi
Singapore | Washington DC | Melbourne

SAGE Publications Ltd
1 Oliver's Yard
55 City Road
London EC1Y 1SP

SAGE Publications Inc.
2455 Teller Road
Thousand Oaks, California 91320

SAGE Publications India Pvt Ltd
B 1/I 1 Mohan Cooperative Industrial Area
Mathura Road
New Delhi 110 044

SAGE Publications Asia-Pacific Pte Ltd
3 Church Street
#10-04 Samsung Hub
Singapore 049483

Editor: Matthew Waters
Editorial assistant: Jasleen Kaur
Production editor: Katherine Haw
Copyeditor: Neville Hankins
Proofreader: Clare Weaver
Indexer: Charmian Parkin
Marketing manager: George Kimble
Cover design: Lisa Harper-Wells
Typeset by: C&M Digitals (P) Ltd, Chennai, India
Printed in the UK

Library of Congress Control Number: 2019937999

British Library Cataloguing in Publication data

A catalogue record for this book is available from
the British Library

ISBN 978-1-5264-6441-5
ISBN 978-1-5264-6442-2 (pbk)

At SAGE we take sustainability seriously. Most of our products are printed in the UK using responsibly sourced
papers and boards. When we print overseas we ensure sustainable papers are used as measured by the
PREPS grading system. We undertake an annual audit to monitor our sustainability.

contents

titles in the series

about the series

Every news bulletin carries stories which relate in some way to the social sciences – most obviously politics, economics and sociology but also, often, anthropology, business studies, security studies, criminology, geography and many others.

Yet despite the existence of large numbers of academics who research these subjects, relatively little of their work is known to the general public. There are many reasons for that but one, arguably, is that the kinds of formats that social scientists publish in, and the way in which they write, are simply not accessible to the general public.

The guiding theme of this series is to provide a format and a way of writing which addresses this problem. Each book in the series is concerned with a topic of widespread public interest, and each is written in a way which is readily understandable to the general reader with no particular background knowledge.

The authors are academics with an established reputation and a track record of research in the relevant subject. They provide an overview of the research knowledge about the subject, whether this be long-established or reporting the most recent findings; widely accepted or still controversial. Often in public debate there is a demand for greater clarity about the facts, and that is one of the things the books in this series provide.

However, in social sciences, facts are often disputed and subject to different interpretations. They do not always, or even often, 'speak for themselves'. The authors therefore strive to show the different interpretations or the key controversies about their topics, but without getting bogged down in arcane academic arguments.

Not only can there be disputes about facts but also there are almost invariably different views on what should follow from these facts. And, in any case, public debate requires more of academics than just to report facts; it is also necessary to make suggestions and recommendations about the implications of these facts.

Thus each volume also contains ideas about 'what we should do' within each topic area. These are based upon the authors' knowledge of the field but also, inevitably, upon their own views, values and preferences. Readers may not agree with them, but the intention is to provoke thought and well-informed debate.

Chris Grey, Series Editor

Professor of Organization Studies

Royal Holloway, University of London

about the author

Jonathan Portes is Professor of Economics and Public Policy at King's College London. His current research concentrates on the economic implications of Brexit and on issues related to immigration and labour mobility, both within the European Union and outside. Other research interests include labour markets, fiscal policy, social security and welfare, and the use of evaluation and evidence in public policy.

He started his career at HM Treasury in 1987, and spent most of his career as a civil servant, serving as Chief Economist at the Department for Work and Pensions from 2002 to 2008 and Chief Economist at the Cabinet Office from 2008 to 2011. He led the Cabinet Office's economic analysis and economic policy work during the financial crisis and on the G20 London Summit in April 2009. In 2011 he became Director of the National Institute of Economic and Social Research.

introduction

Immigration to the UK over the last two decades has run at historically unprecedented levels, altering the face of our society and economy. About 1 in 7 of us were born abroad, up from less than half that at the turn of the century. As a result, immigration has become a deeply contentious political issue, with many arguing it was the main driving force behind the Brexit vote.

But the UK's situation is not unique. Although the historic and political contexts are very different, immigration as an important driver of both economic and social change has become central to recent political developments in the United States and across continental Europe. From the election of Donald Trump to the 2015–16 refugee crisis, immigration has shaped the public debate – and will continue to shape the future of our countries on multiple dimensions.

What are the causes and consequences – economic and social – of immigration? In this short book, I focus on the UK, but my analysis draws on research from many other countries. I begin with a brief history of immigration to the UK, which is inevitably both selective and subjective. Although recent immigration levels are indeed far higher than anything we have ever seen before, I explain why the UK has long been a country shaped in many ways by immigration and immigrants, and that political controversy over (and hostility to) immigration is anything but new.

I next discuss what we know – and do not know – about the impact of immigration. I focus on the economics, partly because that is my subject, and partly because the economic impacts are much easier to quantify and analyse in the short term at least. Does immigration reduce job opportunities for those of us who were born here? Does immigration push down wages? What is the impact of immigration on public finances and public services? What has been the impact of free movement of people both in the UK and the rest of the EU?

The fact that we can speak with more certainty about these economic impacts does not, however, mean that wider social impacts are less important. What do we know about the relationship between immigration, diversity and social cohesion? Why is public opinion in the UK generally hostile to immigration, despite the general consensus among economists that it makes us richer?

Finally, I consider what conclusions we can draw from all of this for the future. I look at areas that are high on the agenda for UK politicians and the public. Brexit will herald the largest shakeup of UK immigration policy in at least 40 years. What should a post-Brexit immigration system look like? How do we shape a public and political consensus for a post-Brexit system based on a better public understanding of the costs, benefits and trade-offs inherent in different options? And what, if anything, do we need to promote integration?

Overall, it is a safe bet that immigration will remain a key political issue in the UK and beyond. I argue that Brexit, under any of the numerous scenarios that might play out over the next few years, gives us a chance to change the terms of debate for the better, though it does not give us any clear answers. We have a chance to reframe both the debate and policy constructively; failure to do so could be very damaging indeed. This book therefore is intended as my contribution to a better outcome.

Concepts, definitions and impacts

Before moving on to the main discussion, it is helpful to say a little about what I mean by 'immigration' and the effects, direct and indirect, that will be discussed in this book. People have been migrating from the dawn of history, moving in search of a better life, whether that means more plentiful game, more fertile land, job opportunities, or fleeing danger or war. We all trace our ancestry back to Africa, and in this sense all countries are the result of immigration and we are all immigrants or their descendants. But of course that far exceeds the scope of this book. To make sense of a contemporary discussion of immigration, we will need a more focused definition, and in such a contentious debate, definitions are neither neutral nor uncontested. For example, some argue that 'free movement' in the EU – the legal right to move from one EU member state to another – is similar to movement within a nation state and is qualitatively different from 'immigration' from outside the EU. The recent Windrush scandal has seen the UK government deport long-term UK residents as part of its 'hostile environment' policy for people who cannot show they have a legal right to residence, even though they were born in countries that were once part of the British Empire and they are, and have always been, entitled to British citizenship.

Without ignoring these issues, I will generally follow the dictionary definition of immigration, which is the 'movement of people from one country to another'. This is operationalised for statistical purposes by the United Nations and the OECD as 'someone who moves from one country to another, intending to stay for more than a year', so as to exclude travel for tourism, business trips, and so on. However, these boundaries are of course blurred in practice, most obviously in the case of seasonal or temporary migrant workers.

This definition excludes some hugely significant, both economically and historically, movements of people within countries, for example the 'Great Migration' of African-Americans from southern to northern states of the United States and that of hundreds of millions of Chinese, mostly from inland agricultural regions to the more industrialised and prosperous coastal provinces. Also, while migration is often not entirely voluntary, some choice over the decision to migrate or where to migrate is generally involved. So I also exclude the transatlantic slave trade which, while involving the movement of people from one country to another and being of enormous historical significance, was not what we normally mean by immigration.

Why do people move? Most obviously, for economic reasons (positive or negative) to take up a specific job, to take advantage of economic opportunity more generally or to escape high unemployment or poverty in their country of origin. These were the key drivers behind, for example, the large-scale movement of Europeans to the Americas in the nineteenth century. But people also choose to move for broader reasons such as education (usually temporary, but can often become permanent), or for family reasons, such as to join a spouse or other family members. There is also forced migration involving political persecution, war (especially civil war) and 'ethnic cleansing'. The boundaries between these different categories are often blurred, which in turn poses a problem for policy and makes it much easier to deal with cases that can be easily and clearly categorised.

Since labour is a factor of production – probably the most important factor of production in both classical and Marxist economics – the movement of people on a large scale is likely to have very significant economic effects. It directly reduces labour supply in the source country and increases it in the destination one. The economic impacts will be strongest for the immigrants themselves, but will also impact others, in particular workers already resident in the destination country.

But this is only part of the story, as we will discover later on. Perhaps the most important concept in the economics of immigration is the 'lump of labour fallacy'. While immigration does increase labour supply, it is simply wrong to claim, as many do, that it must in turn reduce wages or job opportunities for non-immigrants by the laws of supply and demand. In a functioning economy and labour market, immigrants, directly or indirectly, add to labour demand as well as labour supply; they earn money and spend it. So I will focus very much on what the data actually says about the overall effects. Moreover, labour market impacts are by no means the whole story. Large-scale immigration is likely to affect almost all other economic outcomes too: growth, productivity, public finances, and so on.

Immigrants are not just workers. They are also, first and foremost, people. So the broader impacts of immigration are just as important, if not more so, than the economic ones, even if we can be less definitive. Immigration will increase population size and, usually, diversity – not just ethnic but across a number of other dimensions also. Even more controversially, immigration is likely to change a country's culture and identity in unpredictable ways. So over the long term, different levels and patterns of immigration will affect almost everything about how a country develops. This is easy enough to see from history if we compare the very different economic, social and cultural trajectories followed by the United States, Australia, Argentina and Greenland, for example.

These economic and social impacts will, in turn, have political implications. Immigration is usually, but not always, unpopular with large proportions of the resident population, even where that resident population is descended in large part from relatively recent immigrants. It is unclear why that is the case, or what drives attitudes in different countries, but there is plenty of evidence that the political attitudes to immigration reflect at least in part systematic misperceptions of its scale and impacts. Much depends on the speed and nature of assimilation or integration. Immigrants, or their children, eventually get to vote too.

Looking forward, the longer term drivers of immigration are not going to go away and, if anything, are likely to intensify. Demographic pressures involve both supply (very large numbers of young people in developing countries, especially in some African countries with limited job opportunities) and demand sides (low fertility rates and ageing populations in most developed countries). Armed conflicts, particularly civil wars or endemic violence in 'failed states', will continue to drive refugee flows in unpredict-able ways. In addition to these, climate change may result in further large forced movements in the medium to long term.

Finally, before moving on to the main discussion, a personal note. Immigration is an emotive topic and our attitudes are inevitably shaped by our own backgrounds and histories. I am an empirical economist – I work with evidence and data. As best I can, in what follows I summarise accurately and objectively the evidence and analysis that we have on the impacts of immigration. My views on what immigration means for jobs, wages, and so on, are based on that evidence and are aligned with the overwhelming consensus of economists working in this field. But I make no claims to objectivity overall. My parents and my partner's parents were immigrants to this country, as are many of my extended family and friends. I am a Londoner, a city that has in my view benefited hugely from immigration over the half century I have been living here. So bear this in mind as we now move on to discuss the history of immigration to the UK, from the Norman Conquest to the present day.

background

In this chapter, I will give a brief and selective overview of immigration to the UK (history may be too grand a word). Rather than being comprehensive, I have focused on episodes which I think cast some light, directly or indirectly, on today's debates. For a more in-depth read, I would recommend Robert Winder's *Bloody Foreigners: The Story of Immigration to Britain*.

At the risk of belabouring the obvious, the UK is a country of immigration. The myth of a genetically and culturally homogeneous 'white' population, to which was added a Jewish element in the late nineteenth and early twentieth centuries, and a non-white element after the Second World War, is worse than just an oversimplification: it is positively misleading. The UK has always been relatively open and the UK population is now, as it always has been, the result of successive influxes of immigrants and the racial and cultural intermixture of those immigrants with those already there.

It is also reasonably clear, though impossible to quantify, that the UK has benefited considerably in both economic and cultural terms as a result. In retrospect, those benefits are widely accepted. Few (even those who do not have some Jewish or Huguenot ancestry!) would dispute that the Huguenots and the Jews have made major contributions to the UK economy and society. Indeed, there is by now even a welcome degree of consensus that the UK has benefited from post-war immigration from the New Commonwealth, and the current economic consensus is that over the past 20 years migration has, overall, been broadly positive for the UK economy across a range of outcomes and indicators.

However, those benefits were rarely recognised at the time. We may pride ourselves in retrospect on our hospitality towards Jewish refugees, at the turn of the century and during the Nazi era; in fact, the actual record was mixed at best and positively shameful in some respects. Similarly, blatantly racist attitudes towards immigrants from the New Commonwealth came not just from extremists or working-class communities, but from politicians and policy makers at the highest level. Most recently, the economic benefits did not prevent the UK from voting for Brexit, in a large part because of the association of EU membership with free movement and high levels of inward EU migration.

With Brexit we are now moving into a new phase. Will the relative openness of recent years be perceived as a historical aberration? Or will it continue in a different form, as Brexit throws into even sharper relief what is required to make a success of 'global Britain' outside the EU?

Public or popular discussion of immigration in the UK often appears to assume that large-scale immigration is a new phenomenon that began after the Second World War, or even after the expansion of the EU in 2004, and that therefore it is possible to choose a date at which the British Isles were populated only by 'indigenous' inhabitants, and to describe everybody who arrived after that date, or their descendants, as non-indigenous.

For example, in 1999, the then leader of Kent County Council wrote to the Minister for Immigration to complain about the number of asylum seekers, mentioning that Kent had 'no prior history of multicultural diversity'. In fact, Dover itself was represented in Parliament by Thomas Papillon, a Huguenot refugee, back in the seventeenth century. This reflected an ignorance of history rather than malice.

However, such attitudes often either shade into racism or encourage it, even, sadly, in my own profession. More recently, Sir Paul Collier, a development economist who entered the field of immigration studies, wrote in the Daily Mail that 'indigenous Britons' had become a minority in London, 'their own capital' (Collier, 2013). Since this is only true if you restrict the definition of 'indigenous Britons' to white people, he was making an explicit choice to label even second- or third-generation black or mixed-race Britons as somehow foreign, not an attitude that we generally regard as acceptable in current public discourse.

In fact, ever since the British Isles were separated from mainland Europe in approximately 7000 BC, there have been continuous movements of people in and out of these islands. While those associated with conflict are best known, namely the Roman invasion and the raids of the Danes, there was also of course much in the way of trade and commerce. Even before the Roman invasion, there were well-established trade routes linking the British Isles with the Mediterranean. The Celts, who arrived in the first millennium BC, are believed to have originated on the Russian steppes, and so the language(s) spoken here have long been part of the Indo-European family, derived from Sanskrit and which includes Hindi and Punjabi as well as French and Greek.

After the Romans left Britain in the fifth century following the fall of the Roman Empire, there were numerous invasions and armed incursions, first from what is now Germany and the Netherlands (the Angles and the Saxons and others) and later from Scandinavia. King Canute, or Cnut, was a Dane. So by the time of the Norman Conquest in 1066, the population of the British Isles was a mix of Britons, Angles, Saxons, Celts, Danes, and so on – in no particular order and with a great deal of intermixture. The Normans, while intermarrying freely, brought with them perhaps for the first time a distinctive racial/linguistic (as opposed to tribal) identity that took a considerable amount of time to assimilate. Indeed, the tension between the descendants of 'indigenous' Anglo-Saxons and Norman 'invaders' had not completely dissipated even by the seventeenth century, as Christopher Hill notes in *Puritanism and Revolution* (1997).

The Normans and the Jews

The Norman Conquest is an appropriate point at which to commence a discussion of British migration *policy* (as opposed to migration per se) since William the Conqueror invited and encouraged the immigration to England of a substantial number of Jews. This arguably represents the first immigration policy decision taken by an English ruler. His motivations were economic; unlike Christians, Jews were not debarred from usury (moneylending) and were thus able to provide important financial services to the king and ruling elite.

As elsewhere in Christendom, where there were Jews there was also anti-Semitism, arising for both economic and religious reasons. Creditors are rarely loved, and there were the usual legends of ritual murder, as in, for example, Chaucer's *Prioress's Tale*. These in turn provided a convenient excuse for riots or pogroms that could be used violently to write off debts.

There were a number of massacres, notably a riot at the coronation of Richard I in 1189 and shortly afterwards the famous massacre in York, still probably the worst example of anti-immigrant violence in British history.

Matters did not improve over the following century. In 1275, Edward I decreed that Jews should wear a yellow piece of cloth as identification. Like Hitler, Edward did not stop there and the Jews were violently expelled and their property confiscated in 1290. There were probably about 15,000 at this time; not an enormous number, but not insignificant in the context of a total population of no more than 2 million.

Their role in the financial system was largely taken by Italians from Lombardy. But the image of Jews as evil, anti-Christian moneylenders survived in the English consciousness for many centuries after their expulsion. Note that Shakespeare's *Merchant of Venice* and Marlowe's *Jew of Malta* were written at a time when Jews were still not officially allowed into Britain.

The Protestant diaspora

There were continued influxes of Continental Europeans, especially Italians, Flemings (often weavers) and Dutch, through the fourteenth and fifteenth centuries. The state not only welcomed but also encouraged this; Edward III offered immigrant cloth workers protection and tax incentives. But it was the sixteenth and seventeenth centuries that saw a new wave of mass immigration, largely the result of religious persecution of Protestants on the continent. This coincided with (and arguably had much to do with) England's newfound assertiveness as a maritime power and trading nation under Elizabeth I. As now, increasing economic interconnectedness coincided with the violent and bloody manifestation of ethnic, political and religious tensions.

The majority of the newcomers were from France and the Low Countries (now under Spanish rule and hence the Inquisition). Often they too were weavers, and they contributed much to the development of a thriving textile industry, especially in East Anglia. In the last few decades of the sixteenth century, the number arriving amounted to at least 25,000–30,000. By the 1580s, perhaps a third of the population of Norwich was Flemish, Dutch or Walloon. Indeed, the Dutch made a lasting contribution to the landscape of East Anglia – quite literally – when Dutch workers, under the direction of the great engineer Cornelius Vermuyden, drained the Fens, creating the productive arable land that exists there now.

This immigration was by no means a laissez-faire procedure, with refugees simply arriving and settling. There were reception centres where immigrants were screened and then allotted to various areas for settlement. In addition, the occupations in which they could engage were regulated. However, this reflected not a view that the immigrants were generally undesirable, but security concerns on the one hand and the need to take maximum advantage of this economic opportunity on the other. Locally, the immigrants were generally welcomed: the Bailiffs of Colchester petitioned the Privy Council for immigrants, and were content with the results, noting 'how beneficial the strangers of the Dutch congregation have been and are unto our said Towne'.

A further and even larger wave of Protestants, at least 50,000, followed in 1685 with the Revocation of the Edict of Nantes by Louis XIV of France, which protected Protestants from religious persecution. The Huguenots, as they were known, were more dispersed than earlier Protestant refugees, with many going not only to London but also as far as Scotland and Ireland. Like their predecessors, they made important contributions to the textile industry. They also sparked the development of new manufacturing industries like papermaking. More or less contemporaneously, the arrival of William of Orange in 1688 not surprisingly strengthened the already close links, and increased the human interchange, between England and the Netherlands. Meanwhile, the Jews had been allowed to re-establish themselves in 1656 by Oliver Cromwell, and they quickly resumed their position of dominance in finance. Cromwell's conquest of Ireland, while bloody and sectarian, also facilitated economic interchange between the two islands, and there was significant Irish immigration in the eighteenth century.

An age of (relative) tolerance…

The next 200 years did not see influxes on such a scale, although it was in the eighteenth and nineteenth centuries that Britain acquired its reputation as a tolerant place for those whose political views made them unwelcome at home. Many French and other Continental émigrés arrived in the Revolutionary and Napoleonic periods, although many subsequently returned. During the nineteenth century, the long list of significant political figures who took refuge in Britain from repressive Continental regimes includes Garibaldi, Mazzini, Napoleon III, Victor Hugo and Marx, among many others.

Throughout this period there remained no formal controls on immigration. Indeed, by contrast, the Prohibitory Acts imposed significant controls on the *emigration* of artisans which were not fully repealed until the middle of the nineteenth century. This asymmetry reflected the then prevailing economic view of migration. It was generally recognised that Britain and British industry had benefited substantially from the knowledge and human capital brought by the successive waves of immigration described above, and a corresponding view that the country would suffer if skilled craftsmen were allowed to take such human capital abroad.

The assimilation of all these groups was not without problems, but no major social dislocation appeared to result from these population movements. The best known popular disturbances of the eighteenth century, the Gordon Riots, were more anti-Catholic (and anti-government) than anti-Irish. And while the Jews did not assimilate as quickly as other groups, anti-Semitism and institutionalised discrimination were – in contrast to the previous unhappy episode – rather more muted than in most other countries in Europe.

One group, while small, is notable since it was the first to result directly from Britain's maritime predominance, trading prowess and the beginnings of empire, factors which were of course to play such a large role in twentieth-century immigration to the UK. British ships dominated the slave trade and by the end of the eighteenth century there may have been as many as 20,000 black people in Britain, most originally slaves. They made an important contribution to London's cultural life, as well as establishing small but significant communities in Liverpool and Bristol. They intermarried extensively and they had largely been assimilated by the time of the twentieth-century influx of black immigrants.

The Great Migration, 1870–1913

The second half of the nineteenth century, especially the last 25 years, was probably the greatest episode of mass migration the world had ever seen (excluding the slave trade, which was entirely involuntary). Relatively free trade, unrestricted capital movements and sharp falls in transport costs – globalisation, in a word – led, just as economic theory would predict, to huge movements of the factors of production from countries where they were abundant and returns were low to countries where the opposite was the case. For the UK, as for most European countries which were labour-rich and natural resource-poor relative to the New World, this meant primarily emigration (especially from Ireland). Between 1870 and 1913 the British Isles saw net emigration of 5.6 million people, reducing the population by 16% relative to the trend.

But in addition to this economic migration from Europe, there was also a wave of Jewish emigration to the west from Eastern Europe, driven by political persecution rather than (primarily) economics. While the majority of the Jews also crossed the Atlantic to the Americas, several hundreds of thousands came to the UK, with London's Jewish population tripling to more than 150,000. Unlike the bulk of those who had arrived in previous episodes of mass migration to the UK, the Jews were very obviously different in race, religion and culture to the natives. So indeed were the other groups (e.g. Chinese) who began to arrive at this time (albeit in relatively small numbers) as the consequence, one way or the other, of the UK's central economic and political role in the global economy.

The economic environment too was very different; the last two decades of the nineteenth century saw the first Great Depression, near universal male suffrage, the growth of urban slums, and the continued rise of the trade union movement. In contrast to previous arrivals, it was not obvious, at least at the time, that the human capital of this wave would make a net contribution to the UK economy; instead there were fears that it would drive down wages and worsen social conditions in the cities. After all, most migrants were uneducated peasants from the most backward part of Europe, speaking little or no English. In his book *Simiocracy* (1884), the Conservative MP Arthur Greenfield described how a Liberal government extended the franchise to apes, and then perpetuated itself in power by importing millions of African gorillas. This was presumably intended as an attack both on the 1884 Reform Act, which extended the franchise to most adult males, and on immigration.

It was as a reaction to these fears that the first systematic legislative control on immigration in the UK was enacted. For some Conservative

MPs (especially in the East End), the influx of Jews and other East Europeans was a convenient 'wedge issue' which could be used to discredit the Liberals (whose advocacy of free trade extended at least in part to immigration) with the newly enfranchised working class. In a wonderful historical irony, a leading figure here was Mancherjee Bhownaggree, one of the first MPs of Indian origin, who became Conservative MP for Bethnal North-East in East London. His 1895 election leaflet (see Figure 2.1) attributes various negative economic and social developments to immigration, including downward pressure on wages, upward pressure on rents, and so on.

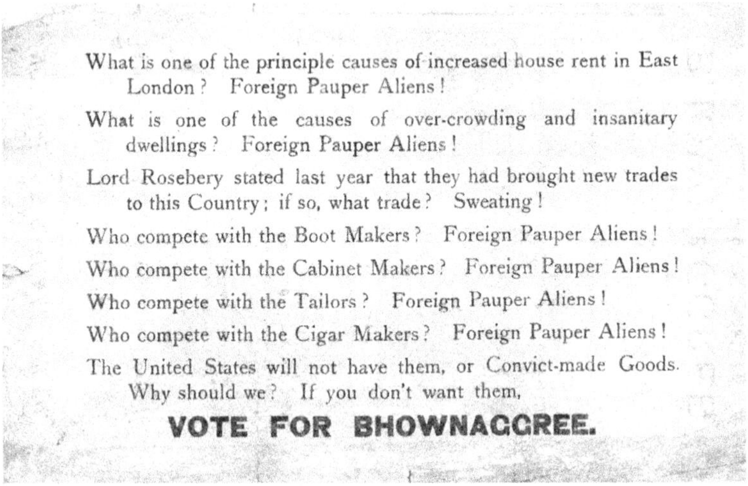

What is one of the principle causes of increased house rent in East London ?   Foreign Pauper Aliens !

What is one of the causes of over-crowding and insanitary dwellings ?   Foreign Pauper Aliens !

Lord Rosebery stated last year that they had brought new trades to this Country; if so, what trade ?   Sweating !

Who compete with the Boot Makers ?   Foreign Pauper Aliens !

Who compete with the Cabinet Makers ?   Foreign Pauper Aliens !

Who compete with the Tailors ?   Foreign Pauper Aliens !

Who compete with the Cigar Makers ?   Foreign Pauper Aliens !

The United States will not have them, or Convict-made Goods. Why should we ?   If you don't want them,

VOTE FOR BHOWNAGGREE.

Figure 2.1

Source: www.ourmigrationstory.org.uk

More than a century later, the UK Prime Minister, Theresa May, expressed very similar sentiments about the supposed impact of low-paid and low-skilled migrants on wages and housing, saying 'we know that for people in low-paid jobs, wages are forced down even further while some people are forced out of work altogether'.

Back in the early twentieth century, the anti-immigration lobby succeeded in establishing a Royal Commission, which called for restrictions. The Alien Immigration Act of 1905, a direct response to Jewish immigration, gave the Home Secretary the power to refuse entry to those who could not support themselves; further legislation followed in 1914, 1919 and 1920. Meanwhile, the First World War then brought the first great era of globalisation and mass migration to an end.

In the 1920s and 1930s, like most other Western countries (and the United States), the UK restricted immigration of Jews and of non-whites, like Chinese. This was explicitly on racial grounds; in particular, it was thought that a further substantial influx of Jews would increase anti-Semitism. This was of course very much the same thinking that drove policy towards non-white immigration after the war. After Hitler took power in 1933, the policy was liberalised somewhat and many more Jews did arrive one way or another as refugees, but there was no generalised right to admission. Many Jews were denied entry; most of these subsequently perished in the concentration camps.

Immigration since the Second World War

International economic migration reappeared after the Second World War. In its immediate aftermath, a substantial further number of East Europeans, either economic or political refugees from newly established communist regimes, settled in the UK. At the same time, the first major influx of economic migrants from British colonies and former colonies began. The beginning of post-war migration from the New, or non-white, Commonwealth is usually identified with the arrival of the *Empire Windrush*, in 1948, carrying Caribbean migrants, many ex-servicemen, to the UK.

As mentioned above, there were of course black people here long before 1945, mostly the descendants of freed slaves and, more recently, of merchant seaman, hence concentrated in ports like Liverpool and Bristol as well as London. There were also significant Chinese communities in some cities. But the total non-white (by contemporary definition) population was relatively small.

The standard conventional wisdom account of immigration to the UK between the war and the 1990s, which focuses on immigrants from the 'New Commonwealth', sees immigration as a succession of 'waves', driven by labour market pressures:

- The 1950s saw a substantial influx of Caribbean immigrants – about 125,000 by 1958.

- Indians (especially Sikhs from the Punjab) arrived in the late 1950s and 1960s, followed by Pakistanis.

- African Asians – mostly Gujaratis who had migrated from India to Kenya and Uganda, when they were all part of the British Empire, migrated again to the UK in the late 1960s and early 1970s, as conditions for Asians in East Africa deteriorated.

- Bangladeshis (especially Sylhetis) in the 1970s and 1980s.

- East European and other asylum seekers in the 1990s, particularly after the wars following the disintegration of Yugoslavia.

- Other nationalities with substantial immigrant flows, often caused by political turbulence in areas that at one point or another had been under British rule, including Cypriots (both Greek and Turkish), Iraqis and Iranians, and Palestinians.

The Alien Immigration Act had never covered subjects of the Crown, including colonial ones, who had always had, in principle, the right to free entry. The Nationality Act of 1948 not only reaffirmed that right but also extended it to the newly independent former colonies, including India, Pakistan and the Caribbean islands. This explains, in part, why many of those who arrived then and were caught up in the UK government's recent crackdown on those suspected of being here illegally could not provide any documentation demonstrating the opposite – they simply assumed that they had the automatic right to reside here, although in fact that right had been removed by subsequent legislation.

Meanwhile, partly in reaction to the experience of the Jews in the Second World War, the UN Convention in 1951 required signatories to grant asylum to those with a 'well-founded fear of persecution'.

However, there was never really free entry for non-white citizens of the Commonwealth. Just as it is a myth that the UK was a tolerant haven for Jews fleeing Nazi persecution, it is also a myth that there was a golden age of colour-blind immigration policy. While entry could not legally be denied, UK officials in the colonies could and did restrict exit; and after independence, the UK government prevailed on India and Pakistan to impose their own restrictions. Jamaica, suffering from high unemployment and with emigration to the rather more attractive United States debarred by the 1952 McCarran Act, was less willing; it was for that reason that the initial post-war immigration surge came from the Caribbean. But it was not necessarily expected that they would stay. The (Labour) Colonial Secretary claimed, 'there's nothing to worry about because they won't last one winter in England'.

The government also did not consistently encourage New Common-wealth migration for labour market purposes. As early as 1953, they looked for ways of excluding immigrants and did not see labour market benefits from 'potentially violent' and 'mentally slow' black people or 'hardworking though unscrupulous' immigrants. Immigration was primarily a market-driven response to supply and demand, rather than a policy-driven one. Only 10% came with the offer of a job. There was no clear correlation between policy and changing labour market conditions, either in the earlier, more liberal period or later as restrictions were progressively tightened.

In fact, policy was driven by social and racial politics as well as economics. Politicians tried to balance, on the one hand, the obligations remaining from empire and, on the other, the (perceived) need for political reasons to stem a (perceived) incipient flood of non-white immigrants.

But it is fair to say that the immigrants from the New Commonwealth were largely welcomed initially, and indeed immigration was positively encouraged because it helped to alleviate labour shortages. The UK in the 1950s and 1960s was booming, with frictional unemployment only. Caribbean immigrants staffed the transport industries and the NHS, which went so far as to advertise for labour in Jamaica with Enoch Powell, then Minister for Health, famously paying a visit to drum up new recruits. Indians and Pakistani immigrants were more dispersed, but made a major contribution – yet again – to the textile industry, this time in the north of the country. Indian doctors also filled GP posts in areas of the country which natives found unattractive.

However, all was not rosy: immigrants faced pervasive racism and discrimination, which meant that they could not necessarily find jobs that reflected their skills. As always, immigrant communities concentrated in certain areas. When those areas, especially urban ones, already faced pressures on housing and schools, racial tensions rose, violently manifesting in the Nottingham and Notting Hill riots of 1958. Popular culture of this time documented these tensions, for example in Shelagh Delaney's play *A Taste of Honey* and Colin McInnes's *Absolute Beginners*.

These tensions took political form also, most notably in the Smethwick election of 1964, where the Conservative candidate, against the national trend, won the seat on the slogan 'If you want a nigger for a neighbour, vote Labour'. This was followed by Enoch Powell's infamous 'Rivers of Blood' speech in nearby Birmingham in 1968, and then gradually by the rise of far-right movements like the National Front and British National Party which were openly racist and campaigned for the compulsory repatriation of immigrants.

The policy result was successively tighter restrictions on immigration from the New Commonwealth, with the Commonwealth Immigrants Acts of 1962 and 1968, rushed through in response to the first wave of arrival of the African Asians, the Immigration Act of 1971 and the British Nationality Act of 1981. These imposed successively tighter restrictions on immigrants from the New Commonwealth, even those with notionally 'British' passports. By 1971 primary immigration from the New Commonwealth had largely come to an end, although dependants continued to be admitted.

However, perhaps 200,000 East African Asians, fleeing Idi Amin as well as less virulent but still anti-Indian regimes in Kenya and elsewhere, who for colonial reasons held British passports, were allowed in effectively, most them arriving as refugees in 1972–3. The decision to admit them was taken by Ted Heath, the Conservative Prime Minister, against considerable opposition both from within his own party and among the general public. Their arrival in the UK was controversial to say the least. *The Daily Telegraph* described how the 'Invasion of Asians Forces Borough to Call for Help'; *The Sun* discussed the 'Storm Over the Two-Wife Migrants'; and the *Daily Mirror* complained about the 'Scandal of Day-Tripper Immigrants'. Some 40 years later, a Conservative minister would point to them as 'one of Britain's greatest success stories' (Warsi, 2012 :18). (See Appendix A: The East African Asians.)

Between this episode and the late 1990s, policy was relatively restrictive towards New Commonwealth immigrants and – it is often argued, as a consequence – less a topic of public debate. Mrs Thatcher, attempting to win back Conservative support lost to the National Front, famously in 1978 expressed sympathy for those who felt 'swamped' by immigrants, but by this time the NF had already peaked. By the 1980s it was marginalised.

So, by the 1990s, many across the political spectrum argued that UK immigration policy had been 'settled' and was no longer a matter of great political concern or controversy. The implicit settlement was the following:

- no more primary non-white immigration and a restrictive but not entirely exclusionary attitude towards family reunion;

- no major changes to or even serious public discussion of the immigration system;

- no repatriation of immigrants or their descendants;

- and (to some extent) the promotion of equal opportunity and anti-racism so as to facilitate the integration and assimilation of non-white immigrants (and their descendants).

Since 1997

All this changed in the late 1990s, although it was not immediately realised at the time. Net migration, which had averaged about 50,000 for the previous decade, rose sharply – tripling in 1997 and continuing its rise thereafter (see Figure 2.2).

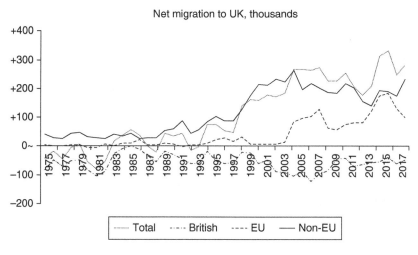

Net migration to UK, thousands

Figure 2.2   Net migration to UK, thousands

Source: Office of National Statistics

There were a number of interrelated drivers. Most fundamental was globalisation. The previous era of globalisation in the late nineteenth century was marked by much higher labour mobility than today (with mass immigration to the United States, Canada and Australia). While there may be theoretical questions as to whether globalisation in terms of trade increases or decreases the economic incentive to migrate, in practice it seems clear that the reduction in transport and transaction costs that is driving globalisation also increases both the incentive and desire to migrate, despite the convergence in wage costs that it also brings.

Economic and political forces are interlinked. As in the sixteenth century, economic globalisation went hand-in-hand with political turmoil and the movement of people. So just as East European Jews towards the end of the last century were both fleeing persecution and seeking a better life, asylum seekers from Sri Lanka, Somalia, Afghanistan and the former Yugoslavia – the largest source countries in 1998 – were at the same time escaping armed conflict (if not necessarily direct, individually targeted persecution) and looking for economic opportunities.

But globalisation also interacted with immigration policy. The Labour government that came to power in 1997 saw a liberal approach to immigration as shoring up its business-friendly credentials, while, in contrast to some trade unions in the United States and some other European countries, the broader labour movement and trade unions were also relatively liberal on this topic. Labour both relaxed rules on family migration and greatly streamlined the work permit system, resulting in large increases for both family and work-related immigration.

At first this relaxation was largely a reaction to external economic and political pressures, but the government quickly realised that immigration was, once again, becoming a significant policy issue. In January 2001, the government published the first attempt to assess the economic and social implications of immigration for the UK, written by a team of civil servants led by myself (Glover et al., 2001). It foreshadowed a number of the debates that continue today, concluding that overall, migration had benefited and would continue to benefit the UK economy and society; that migration was likely, for a number of reasons, to continue to increase; and that policy should be directed not at trying to restrict this increase but rather to manage it and to maximise the benefits. All these propositions remain both relevant and controversial.

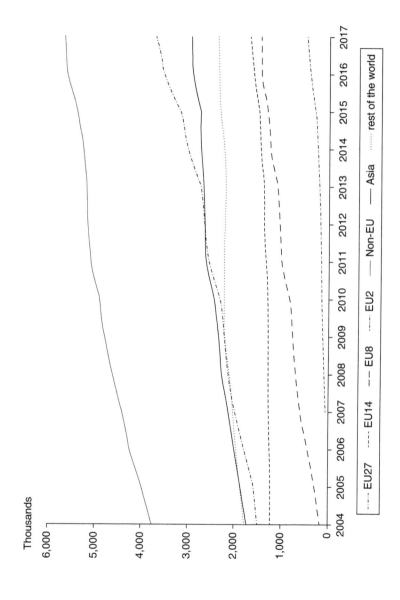

Figure 2.3 Estimation of the non-UK born resident population of the UK by country of birth, 2004 to 2017

Source: Office for National Statistics

EU enlargement and free movement

But the biggest turning point in the recent history of immigration to the UK was the government's decision to give immediate access to the UK labour market to citizens of the new member states of East and Central Europe that joined the EU in 2004. When the UK joined the EU (then called the European Economic Community) in 1973 and subsequently voted to remain a member in 1975, the potential impact on either UK immigration policy, or the level and nature of immigration to the UK, appeared to be relatively small. The accession to the Union of Spain and Portugal in 1986 did not lead to a significant increase in migration flows. Although they had traditionally been countries of emigration, their accession (and large inflows of EU funding) led swiftly to rapid economic growth and ample domestic demand for labour. But given the much larger disparities in economic development between existing member states and those of Central and Eastern Europe, the potential for large migration flows was clearly much greater.

A myth has grown up that the main reason the government granted immediate access was because of a supposed 'Home Office forecast' that only 13,000 migrants would arrive (Dustmann et al., 2003). In fact, this paper, produced by independent external academics, was only a small part of the story. There were three far more important arguments for the decision.

First, the broader geopolitical one. The UK had long been the most vigorous proponent of membership for the countries of the former Eastern Bloc; they were seen (correctly) as likely allies for the UK's generally liberal positions in EU debates. So the decision was seen as a way of cementing the UK's relationship with them and in particular the Polish government.

Second, the economics. The UK labour market was in good shape, and all the analyses suggested that immigrant workers, particularly the reasonably well-educated and motivated ones likely to arrive from the new member states, were likely to boost the UK's economy without doing much if any damage to the prospects of native workers.

And third, the practicalities. Free movement – the right to travel between different EU countries, with only minimal and targeted restrictions – is an absolute right within the EU. So it was not an option for the UK government to prevent the citizens of the new member states from coming here, for example by requiring visas; this would have been illegal. The only option was to forbid them from working legally once here. The assumption within government was that this would lead to a sharp rise in illegal working, which did not seem like an attractive alternative.

The consequences of this decision and subsequent events in Europe have been very large indeed for immigration to the UK. Since 2004, the number of UK residents who were born elsewhere in the EU has risen from about 1.5 million to 3.7 million (see Figure 2.3).

Not only was there a large surge in migration from Eastern and Central Europe in 2004 – which in retrospect was hardly surprising, since the citizens of those countries had had very limited opportunities to migrate, at least legally, before accession – but it also persisted for a number of years. The financial crisis and ensuing recession, which reduced the easy availability of jobs, did temporarily reduce flows to the UK in the 2008–12 period.

However, after 2013, recovery in the UK labour market and continuing economic difficulties in some eurozone countries led to a renewed upsurge in migration flows, with younger people from crisis-hit countries like Spain and Greece, where youth unemployment rose to very high levels, moving in significant numbers. Moreover, Bulgaria and Romania joined the EU in 2007; this time, the UK government did impose transitional controls, but they expired in 2014, and this resulted in a further sharp rise in the migration of EU citizens to the UK. In the year to June 2016, the date of the Brexit referendum, net migration to the UK reached its highest ever level, about 330,000, and polls showed it as the most important single issue in UK politics.

The political implications of this rise in migration were slow to materialise, but eventually seismic. In the 2005 election, the Conservative Party (led by Michael Howard, the son of a Jewish refugee from Romania) produced an election poster that stated: 'It's not racist to impose limits on immigration ... Are you thinking what we're thinking?' Although the Conservatives lost the election, immigration did not go away. It was by no means the central issue in the 2010 election, which was dominated by economic concerns following the financial crisis, but David Cameron did make the ill-advised but politically expedient pledge to reduce net migration to the 'tens of thousands' (it was then running at about 200,000).

The chief problem with this promise, which fell to the then new Home Secretary, Theresa May, to deliver, was that the government controlled some but not all components of the net migration figure. With no control over EU migration or UK citizens entering and leaving the country, it was forced to seek substantial reductions in non-EU migration. Inevitably, this meant a focus on areas where it was relatively easy to reduce numbers, such as skilled workers and students. But equally these were areas where the economic benefits of migration were most obvious and where pressure from employers to maintain a relatively liberal policy was strongest. It soon became apparent that actually meeting the target would require measures which would significantly damage the UK economy.

The result was that no one was happy. The new restrictions did significant damage, both to the affected sectors and to the UK's global reputation (particularly the more clumsy attempts to reduce the number of international students). They did reduce numbers, but by nowhere near enough to meet the target, which became emblematic of the government's perceived lack of 'control'. And as it became increasingly obvious that the main obstacle to further reductions was freedom of movement, the issues of the UK's membership of the EU and immigration became conflated in a way that they never had been previously (immigration had simply not been an issue in the 1975 referendum).

For this reason, David Cameron's 'renegotiation' of the terms of the UK's membership of the EU focused on restricting freedom of movement. When it became clear that he would secure only minimal changes (some restrictions on the rights of EU citizens to claim benefits, but little or nothing to restrict migration per se), the consequences for the referendum campaign were obvious. Negative attitudes to immigration, and in particular free movement within the EU, were an extremely strong predictor of opposition to UK membership.

The Remain campaign tried to avoid any discussion of immigration and free movement at all, while the Leave campaign successfully used the slogan 'Take Back Control' – meaning, most of all, 'control' over the UK's borders. Vote Leave also successfully used the largely meaningless promise of an 'Australian-style points-based system' to claim that it wanted 'controlled' immigration involving fewer unskilled or low-paid workers. The campaign even appealed to some ethnic minority communities by suggesting that reduced access for EU citizens would translate into greater access among, for example, Bangladeshis and Nigerians – although this sentiment was by no means shared by the vast majority of Leave voters.

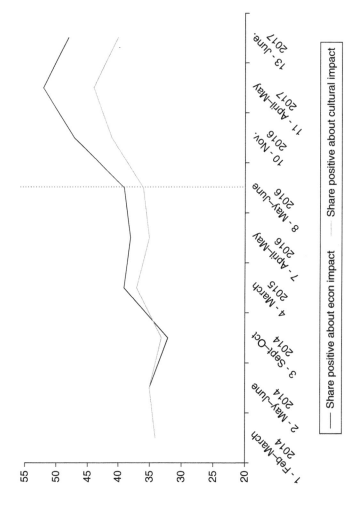

Figure 2.4 Views of economic and cultural impact of immigration (BES panel)

Source: Ford (2018), British Election Survey

Since the 2016 referendum, migration from the EU has fallen sharply. This is not because free movement has ended. Assuming that the UK eventually concludes a withdrawal agreement with the EU, nothing will change in law and policy terms until at least December 2020 and under some circumstances free movement might continue even beyond that. But the vote itself made the UK a less attractive place for Europeans contemplating a move, and other factors such as economic developments in the eurozone, in particular the health of the Polish economy and the fall in the pound, have compounded matters.

In parallel, public attitudes have shifted again: immigration is much less salient as an issue and attitudes are significantly more positive, perhaps as voters realise the broader negative economic consequences of reduced immigration (see Figure 2.4).

Other developments have shown that it is possible for politicians to appear too tough on immigration, particularly when it offends the basic sense of fairness of a majority of the electorate. The recent 'Windrush scandal' saw some of those who arrived in the immediate post-war wave of Caribbean immigration denied access to healthcare, or even deported, because they could not demonstrate their permanent residence status – despite having lived in the UK for four decades or more. This resulted in the appointment of a significantly more liberal Home Secretary. The Cabinet and perhaps the country appear to be split on not one but two key dimensions of future policy: should it be liberal or restrictionist and, separately, should it give preference to European citizens, perhaps as part of our wider post-Brexit relationship with the EU, or should it broadly treat all non-UK citizens on a similar basis?

So while Brexit and the likely – although still not certain – end of free movement will most likely mean a major turning point in UK immigration policy, we are far from clear in which direction. Nearly three years after a referendum in which immigration was the central issue, we actually know less, if anything, about the future of the UK immigration system than we thought we did then. The next few years will be another key moment in the history of UK immigration.

what do we know about immigration? economics

Theory

The essence of the economic case for migration is very simple: it is the same as the case for markets in general. If people take decisions on the basis of their own economic self-interest, this will maximise efficiency and hence overall output and, at least using some measures, welfare. This applies to where people live and work just as much, if not more, as it applies to buying and selling goods and services. Of course markets fail here, as elsewhere, and 'more market' is not always better. But the view that, as a general proposition, markets are good at allocating resources – including human resources – is widely shared among economists. And this analogy holds in a narrower, more technical sense as well. The classic argument for free trade, as advanced by Adam Smith, is not just analogous to, but formally identical to, the argument for free movement. It is easy to see this. In economic terms, allowing somebody to come to your country and trade with you (or work for you, or employ you) is identical to removing trade barriers with their country. It allows greater specialisation – the principle of comparative advantage – and hence greater overall efficiency.

So what then is the impact if a country reduces barriers to trade or migration? Theory suggests that, for both trade and migration, the impact of reducing barriers will be positive but there will be distributional consequences. GDP – and more importantly, GDP per capita, or income per head, for the existing population – will increase, but some individuals and households will lose out, at least in the short term. In particular, trade will hurt those working in sectors where the country does not have a comparative advantage, while immigration will hurt those who are in direct competition with immigrant workers.

Unsurprisingly therefore, much public and policy concern in the UK and other developed countries has focused on the distributional impacts of immigration – the potential negative impacts on employment and wages for low-skilled workers. Many non-economists (and even some economists) simply assert as an article of faith that such effects must exist – usually suggesting that it is a matter of 'supply and demand'. As we will see, this is bad economics.

Jobs and wages

When I first began working on the analysis of migration in the late 1990s, there was virtually no evidence on what impact post-war immigration had had on the UK economy. Indeed, one of the first and most obvious recommendations that I made was that the government should fund and encourage much more research on this topic. That, at least, has happened; and the increasingly obvious importance of immigration to the UK economy and society has meant that the number of researchers working in the field has expanded massively. As a consequence, the evidence base has also grown considerably.

As in other countries, the impact of immigration on the labour market – on the job prospects and wages of native workers – is both a major political issue and a key focus on academic work. So what have we learnt about the impact of two decades of high immigration on British workers?

First, some theory. It seems obvious that if an immigrant takes a job in the UK that there is one less job for a British worker. And in one sense this is true. If the immigrant takes the job, by definition the Brit cannot. But it would be wrong to conclude that the overall level of unemployment goes up; that would only follow if the number of jobs was fixed. This is the so-called 'lump of labour fallacy'. It is also worth noting that this logic would imply that encouraging women to enter the workforce would push up unemployment or that the government could reduce unemployment by forcing people to retire early.

What the lump of labour fallacy misses is that immigration adds to both labour supply and labour demand. If an immigrant gets a job, they will earn money, most of which will be spent. The business they work for may see its profits rise; that money too has to go somewhere. The result is higher demand for goods and services in the economy, and hence higher demand for labour. There is no necessary reason to think unemployment will rise; this will depend on a number of other factors, including both local supply and demand for labour, and whether overall the economy is running at capacity or not.

Over the medium to long run then, almost all economists think that the labour market will adjust to inflows of immigrants: the equilibrium level of unemployment is driven by other things, such as how well the education and training system works and whether the benefit system does a good job of getting unemployed people back to work. And a quick glance at the UK data confirms this (see Figure 3.1). Over the period 1997 to 2017, the proportion of the UK workforce born abroad rose steadily and is now about 17%, but the unemployment rate is now about 4%, the lowest since the mid-1970s.

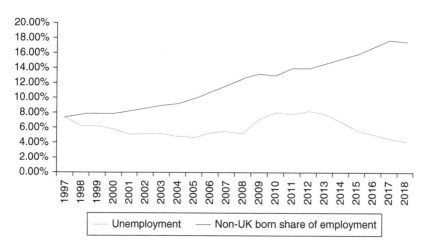

Figure 3.1 Unemployment and migration

Source: Office of National Statistics

This does not mean that immigration could not drive up unemployment in the short run, as the market adjusts; whether it does or not is an empirical question. Answering this question, however, is not easy. The obvious way to do it is to look at areas in the UK where immigration has been high and to compare them with other areas where it has been low. Has unemployment risen, or risen more, in high-immigration areas? In general, no. If anything, the opposite (see Figure 3.2).

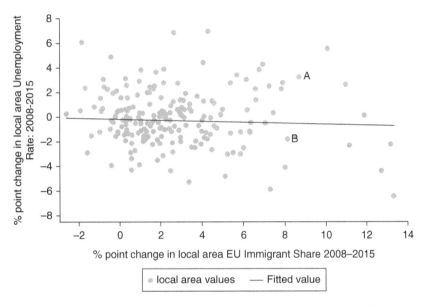

Figure 3.2 Change in UK-born Unemployment Rate 2008–2015

Source: Centre for Economic Performance, London School of Economics

This itself does not prove that immigration does not drive up unemployment. In particular, it is possible that immigrants choose to move to areas where unemployment is low and jobs are easily available or where it is falling. This would distort the chart above – unemployment in high-immigration areas would have been even lower, or fallen even faster, if there had been no immigration. So economists need to use more sophisti-cated techniques to control for other factors and to allow for this so-called 'reverse causality' (meaning that while immigration may increase unem-ployment, unemployment may also reduce immigration). For example, areas that had high immigration in the past tend to have high immigration now, regardless of whether or not their labour markets are performing well. So, if we look at those areas and find that unemployment is rising faster, this might suggest that current levels of immigration are part of the reason.

And there is now quite an extensive set of research results on this topic for the UK. The conclusions are pretty clear: if there are any impacts at all, even in the short run, they are not very big. As the government's independent Migration Advisory Committee concluded in its report on the impact of EU migration on the UK economy, 'there is little or no impact of immigration on the employment or unemployment of existing workers' (Migration Advisory Committee, 2018).

What about wages? Again, it is easy to make a simple, indeed simplistic, argument that says 'More workers mean lower wages. It's just supply and demand.' And again, it is true that when looked at in isolation, an increase in labour supply holding labour demand constant will reduce wages; but immi-gration is also likely to increase labour demand. It is also plausible in theory that more workers for the same amount of capital will increase returns to capital (profits) while reducing average wages; but over time, this will in turn increase the incentive to invest, pushing wages back up again. So, while there may be some short-term impacts, there is no reason to believe that immigration will depress wages overall on a sustained basis.

But what about the common-sense argument that when there are more people looking for work, employers can get away with paying less? Here it is important to distinguish between nominal wages (wages in cash terms) and real wages (adjusted for inflation). Suppose a shortage of workers (resulting from lower immigration or any other factor) does push up the wages employers have to offer. If nothing else changes (i.e. if the amount each worker produces on average does not change) then overall incomes will have gone up in cash terms, but the amount the economy produces will not. Inflation will rise and real wages, which are ultimately driven by what workers can produce, will fall back to their original level. Alternatively, higher immigration may lead to lower pay rises in cash terms, but will also lead to lower inflation and hence the same level of real wages.

However, while immigration may not have much sustained impact on overall wages, it is more plausible that it could affect relative wages. If immigration boosts the number of low-skilled workers, this could push down their wages, while also pushing down the prices of goods and services they produce. They would suffer, but high-skilled workers would benefit, both from reduced prices and, perhaps, because the easier availability of low-skilled workers might make high-skilled workers more productive and hence boost their wages.

For most of the post-war period, real wages for UK workers grew steadily, usually by 1.5% to 2% a year or so. Over the last decade, they have hardly increased at all; this is historically unprecedented. But it is very difficult to put this down to immigration; the main cause was clearly the financial crisis of 2008 and its aftermath, particularly the sustained period

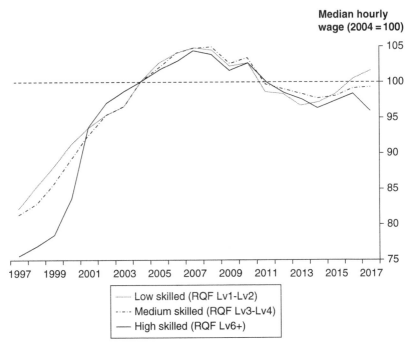

Figure 3.3 UK-born median gross hourly wage by occupational skill level, 2016 prices (2004 = 100)

Source: Migration Advisory Committee (2018)

of very low productivity growth. Indeed, in general, the worst periods for real wage growth (the immediate aftermath of the crisis, and more recently the immediate aftermath of the Brexit vote) have also coincided with periods of falling immigration.

Most striking in this context is the fact that low-skilled workers have not fared worse since the large increase in migration of lower paid workers from the EU after 2004 (see Figure 3.3). If anything, they have done rather better than medium- and high-skilled workers over the last few years, presumably because of large increases in the National Minimum Wage.

As with unemployment, however, it is necessary to dig deeper into the data to work out what the real impact of immigration is. In particular, the fact that wages are weak when immigration is falling is likely to reflect the fact that lower wages make the UK less attractive as a destination. And here the evidence is more mixed. Overall, while it does not look as if immigration has had much if any impact on average wages, it may have depressed wages for some workers, particularly lower paid or low-skilled ones. These impacts do not appear to be very large: for example, an analysis by the Bank of England found that a 1 percentage point rise in the proportion of migrant workers in the low-skilled service sector led to a fall in wages for UK-born workers in that sector of 0.12% (Nickell and Saleheen, 2015). While this was often cited during the Brexit campaign as proof that freedom of movement was indeed hurting low-paid British workers, the author himself, the eminent economist Professor Steve Nickell, dismissed this impact as 'infinitesimal'.

Studies like these, because of limitations in the statistics, tend to look only at very broad groups of workers such as the 'low-skilled'. It is much more plausible to think that immigration could have big impacts on the wages of much smaller groups of workers who face particularly intense immigrant competition. Even there, however, the evidence is not as clear as might be expected. For example, construction, especially in London, is frequently cited as a sector where EU migration, in particular, has been very high. And it has: Figure 3.4 shows that the proportion of self-employed construction workers in London who originate from the new member states of the EU has risen from close to zero to more than half – truly a dramatic change. But if there has been a big impact on the earnings of self-employed UK-born construction workers, they are certainly not telling the taxman; their earnings relative to the national average have gone up, not down, over this period.

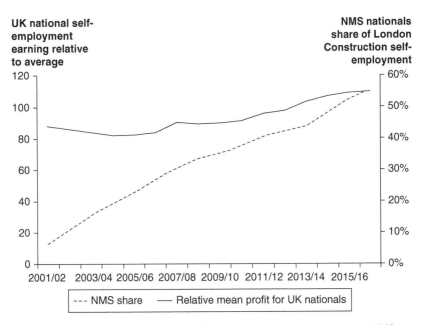

Figure 3.4 Self-employment earnings of UK nationals relative to average vs NMS share of self-employment – London construction sector (2001/02 – 2016/17)

Source: Migration Advisory Committee (2018)

Productivity and growth

But the impacts of immigration on the economy go beyond the direct impacts on the jobs and wages of natives. The economic impacts of trade are not just about reduced prices for consumers for cheap imports; they also include increased competition, technology transfer, the development of multinational supply chains, and so on. Similarly, in recent years there has been increasing interest in other ways in which immigration affects the economy. For example, there is a considerable body of evidence that suggests that immigration is associated with increased innovation (e.g. that immigrants are more likely to register patents and that this, in turn, leads to an increase in patent activity on the part of natives). Immigration is also associated with international trade and knowledge transfer, particularly in high-tech industries (Nathan, 2014).

In particular, could immigration push up productivity and hence (per capita) growth? Put another way, does adding to the population through immigration increase not only the size of the economy but average incomes and living standards as well? This might seem counterintuitive, particularly if immigrants are less skilled than natives, or more likely to work in lower productivity jobs. But there are a number of mechanisms by which migration could increase productivity. In particular, immigrants' skills or the jobs that they are prepared to do may complement those of natives, improving the functioning of the economy across the board. For example, in Italy, it appears that low-skilled migration increased the labour force participation of highly skilled native women, presumably because the migrants performed services (childcare or domestic labour) that allowed women who would otherwise have had to remain at home to go out to work (Barone and Mocetti, 2011). Alternatively, if low-skilled migrants increase the incentives for natives to move jobs or to acquire more skills, this may improve rather than reduce their employment opportunities and wages; researchers have found these effects in both the United States and Europe.

And it does appear that countries with higher levels of immigration do, other things equal, see faster growth as a result. A recent analysis by researchers at the International Monetary Fund found that a 1% increase in the migrant share of the adult population results in an increase in GDP per capita and productivity of approximately 2% (Jaumotte et al., 2016). Perhaps surprisingly, the estimated aggregate impacts of high- and low-skilled migration are not significantly different. The distributional implications, however, are quite different – people with higher incomes gain more from low-skilled migration.

Immigrants are not homogeneous – it matters who they are, where they come from, and what skills and other attributes they have. Both economic theory and common sense would suggest this means that skilled immigrants would be more beneficial than unskilled ones and that immigrants who were selected or chosen by the country of immigration would be more beneficial than others like refugees or those who move for family reasons. But the empirical evidence is less clear on this than might be expected. As the discussion above shows, there are circumstances in which unskilled immigration can also be positive – because it fills specific gaps in the labour market, or is complementary to higher skilled natives, enabling the economy as a whole to function more efficiently.

Moreover, while it may appear attractive for governments to say that they want to manage immigration policy so that a country only gets the immigrants it 'needs' (usually skilled immigrants), in practice that is harder than it sounds. No system can select perfectly, or even close to it. It is surprisingly hard to work out just from someone's educational background or paper qualifications how well they will do in a new country. Governments are not very good at economic planning in general and certainly not when it comes to labour markets. And – a point that is often missed in domestic political debates – it ignores the fact that migration is not just a matter of a country choosing its immigrants; the immigrants have to choose the country.

Nevertheless, most countries do give highly skilled migrants preferential treatment. Australia, Canada and New Zealand are often singled out as high-immigration countries with strong preferences for more skilled or educated immigrants. These systems seem to work reasonably well – certainly better than that of the United States – and, crucially, command a reasonable degree of political consensus. But even these systems are somewhat hit and miss, with the labour market performance of recent immigrants to all these countries not matching the educational qualifications of those migrants. By contrast, in the UK, migration from the rest of the EU – which, under the current free movement rules, is not planned, managed or selected by the UK government – has resulted in a mix of migrants which is nevertheless relatively highly skilled, even compared with the aforementioned countries, and who seem to have little difficulty finding or keeping jobs.

What is certain is that the 'productivity puzzle', the UK's abysmal level of productivity growth, is perhaps the UK's most serious long-term economic problem. Indeed, over the past decade, productivity has hardly grown at all, in sharp contrast to most of the post-war period when it rose steadily. Many people have argued that EU migration is likely to have depressed productivity growth, either through a simple 'batting average' effect (since new EU migrants are on average paid less than the average of the current workforce) or, more tenuously, because the availability of relatively low-paid but flexible workers reduces the incentive to invest in labour-saving and/or productivity-enhancing equipment. For example, people point to the reappearance of manual car washes, often staffed by immigrants, rather than automatic ones; and the fact that much agricultural work, especially fruit-picking, is still done by hand.

But these sectors are relatively small and there are plenty of counter-examples (few would dispute that immigration has pushed up productivity in the higher education sector). A look at the data overall does not point to immigration as the main culprit: the fall in productivity coincides with the financial crisis and its aftermath (which of course in turn led to a fall in migration) rather than the earlier sharp rise in migration. The sharpest fall in productivity has been in the financial sector, which again seems unlikely to be directly the result of immigration.

However, there is much less evidence on productivity than on jobs and wages. As part of its research into the economic impacts of immigration, the Migration Advisory Committee commissioned research on the impact of migration on productivity in the UK. Three separate papers – including one authored by myself – looked at the impact of recent immigration to the UK, by local authority, sector and region. We all found that overall higher levels of immigration were associated with substantially higher, not lower, productivity. Indeed, my paper found a very similar impact to that found by the IMF research described above (Campo et al., 2018).

This research is far from conclusive. Even if, as seems likely, immigration, especially high-skilled immigration, does overall improve UK productivity, we still do not know through which of the possible mechanisms described above this happens. And it is still possible that in some sectors some types of immigration do have negative effects. We can be fairly confident, however, that sharp cuts in immigration, far from helping the UK solve its productivity problem, would do more harm than good.

Public finances and public services

From the point of view of the resident population, perhaps the most obvious impact of immigration is on public services. Immigrants use public transport, they fall ill and their children attend schools. They may also claim welfare benefits – although in most countries immigrants are not entitled to the same benefits as citizens, at least not until they have been in the country for a set amount of time. But these services are themselves funded out of tax revenue and immigrants also pay taxes. So the question of whether immigration improves or reduces the quality of public services for natives depends primarily on whether they cost more than they contribute.

Since much, if not all, immigration is for work purposes and immigrants are generally likely to be relatively young, it might be expected that they would indeed pay more in tax than they take out in public services. Looking at the UK, this does appear to be the case: research, also for the Migration Advisory Committee, showed that the overall fiscal contribution of all immigrants living in the UK in 2016 was slightly higher than that of natives (Oxford Economics, 2018). But this masks huge variation within the immigrant (and indeed the native) population. People in work, higher earners and single people are much more likely to make a net contribution while those who are not working (especially the retired) and those with young children are much less likely to do so.

While immigrants overall may pay in more than they take out, this clearly is not true of each and every immigrant. Nor is it true of every individual citizen. Indeed, the entire point of the welfare state is to redistribute – from the better off to the worse off, from workers to the old, from the healthy to the sick, and so on. But, from the point of view of the general public, different rules seem to apply here for immigrants than citizens – hence concerns about 'benefits tourism' and 'health tourism'. There is in fact, however, very little evidence that any significant numbers of people choose to migrate because they think they will have access to more generous welfare benefits or better public services – certainly not to the UK (Giulietti, 2014).

Research also finds a large disparity between EU migrants, who made a large positive contribution, and those from elsewhere, whose contribution was negative. This might seem counterintuitive, since the UK government has much less control over EU migrants than non-EU ones; it reflects the fact that EU migrants have very high employment rates and are on average younger (and have been in the country less time) so are less likely to have children or to be retired.

However, simply looking at the contribution of all immigrants at a specific point in time does not necessarily tell us that much. Most of us cost the state money when we are children, pay in when we are working and then take out again when we are retired. So it is hardly surprising that young migrants in employment make an initial positive fiscal contribution; to make a proper assessment of the impact of allowing people to move here requires us to look at their contribution not just now but in the future. Doing this, the same research gives us a similar but more positive picture. Looking at immigrants who arrived in the UK in 2016 and estimating what will happen to them over time (progress in work, retire, get sick, return to their home countries), both EU and non-EU migrants are expected to make large positive contributions, totalling about £25 billion in 2016 over their lifetimes. In other words, the (high by historical standards) level of immigration in 2016 will help the government finance public services not just now but for some years to come (and, correspondingly, sharp cuts in immigration would be likely to require tax rises or public service cuts).

Just looking at the national level does not necessarily correspond to how immigration affects public services at a local level. If funding allocations do not adjust quickly enough to population change, then the impact, real and perceived, of increased demand will be negative. A notable recent example is the shortage of primary school places in some parts of the UK (especially London). This appears to be largely the result of poor planning on the part of central government, given the rise in the number of young children resulting from recent increases in migration (from both the EU and elsewhere).

But broader concerns about the potential negative impacts on public services appear to be largely unsubstantiated. There are many anecdotal claims about people finding it harder to get access to NHS services because of too many immigrants also seeking treatment. At a national level, the broader impact of immigration is to increase rather than decrease the funding available per person, but it is certainly plausible that an influx of immigrants to specific areas could increase waiting times. But this does not seem to be what happens in practice; in fact, areas with higher levels of immigration did not see higher waiting times as a result (Giuntella et al., 2018). It seems likely that increases in waiting times simply reflect broader pressures on the NHS resulting from spending constraints.

The impact of immigration on the demand for health services is mostly simply about having more people. But for schools it is more complex and not just about supply and demand; it is about how immigration changes the nature of the school. The children of migrants, who may be from very different backgrounds from natives, may impact on the character and quality of education for everyone, even if the amount of money per pupil is unchanged. This could go either way: on the one hand, if teachers are having to deal with classes in which many children do not speak English well, or have no background in the UK education system, they may have less time for other children. On the other hand, a more diverse group of pupils may learn from each other, and it is often argued that immigrants have higher educational aspirations for their children, which may help raise aspirations and standards across the board.

Here two striking facts about the UK education system are relevant. First, pupils from most ethnic minority backgrounds do fairly well – and, taking account of their parents' income and socio-economic status, extremely well. Second, the remarkable improvement of the relative performance of London schools compared with the rest of the country. These are fairly recent developments, beginning in the 2000s, and in both respects the UK experience differs very sharply to that of almost all other developed countries.

It is impossible to attribute these trends directly to immigration, but clearly there is some relationship. Nor is there any evidence that non-migrant pupils have suffered as a result: a detailed school-level analysis failed to find any strong link between the proportion of pupils for whom English was not their first language and the performance of those for who it was. If anything, the impact was slightly positive (Geay et al., 2013).

But although there is little or no evidence of negative impacts from migration on public services, this does not mean that citizens do not associate their experience of deterioration in public service quality and availability from other factors. In particular, it is hardly surprising that many voters associated the cuts in funding during the UK's ongoing fiscal consolidation programme with the increased demand resulting from higher levels of immigration, particularly since some politicians went out of their way to say just that. The fact that migrants' fiscal contribution could, in principle at least, provide enough funding to cover their marginal impact on demand is not much comfort in practice if those revenues are in fact being allocated elsewhere, for tax cuts or deficit reduction, as has been the case since 2010 in the UK.

This shifting of the blame, from political decisions on the allocation of resources to immigration, can have real political impacts. While the result of the Brexit referendum clearly reflected in large part attitudes to immigration and free movement, there was little or no correlation between the strength of the Leave vote at local level and immigration. Meanwhile, several analyses have shown an association with spending reductions. Both reductions in funding from central government to local authorities – resulting in turn to cuts to local services – and specific changes to the benefits system appear to be associated with rises in support for the UK Independence Party (UKIP) which in turn was associated with the Brexit vote. Given the media coverage of immigration, as well as the voices of some influential politicians, it is hardly surprising some voters concluded that immigrants were a burden on the welfare state and public services.

Population, housing and congestion

Does immigration make the UK a more crowded and congested place? At one level, the answer is obvious. UK population growth has been relatively rapid in recent years, and while this is partly due to increased life expectancy and some upturn in fertility rates, it largely reflects immigration, directly and indirectly, and growth is expected to continue, with the population forecast to hit 70 million around 2030 or so. But simplistic observations that England is a small, overcrowded country, or that 'we are full' don't make much sense. In fact, only about 7% of the UK's land area is 'urban' – and well under half of that is actually built on. By contrast, more of the UK is woodland than at any time since records began a century ago. Nor does increased population necessarily translate to environmental degradation in other respects. Despite population growth, our carbon dioxide emissions are now lower than they were at any time in the last 130 years.

But what about London, where the impacts of immigration on density are most obvious? London's population is now at record levels, but this conceals a massive shift. Islington (where I live) is the most densely populated local authority in the country, but it is still far less crowded than it was in 1939. The same is true of most of Inner London. London has spread out, and is not actually that densely populated by the standards of very large cities.

And while there is no denying the impact of increasing population on transport, traffic and the like, it should not be forgotten that the alternative could be much worse. I arrived in London in the early 1970s; inner London's population shrunk by fully 20% in that decade. It's easy for today's Londoners, living in one of the world's great global cities, to forget that only 30-odd years ago London (like New York) faced falling population, rising crime, and no obvious replacement for vanishing manufacturing jobs; it seemed doomed to permanent decline. Overall, the balance sheet looks highly positive.

There is, however, little doubt that recent immigration has pushed up house prices, especially in London and the South-East, although there is no consensus on how large the impact has been, and most estimates suggest that it has not been the main driver. While the underlying cause here is the dysfunctional nature of the UK housing market – other countries manage to build new houses much more quickly and efficiently than we do – this is little comfort to those who find themselves paying more to buy or rent, or priced out entirely of the area they'd like to live. Here the main impact of immigration may be redistributive within the UK population, since those who currently own property gain from rising prices and rents, while others lose.

Conclusion

The rapid growth in immigration to the UK has been accompanied by a huge expansion in the research evidence on its economic impacts. On some issues, there is considerable consensus – immigration simply has not had the negative impacts on jobs or wages that some feared (and some continue to claim). Overall, it has been broadly positive for the public finances and hence for public services, although at the same time it may have contributed to local pressures, and to higher house prices. However, there is less agreement about the wider economic impacts, which are inherently difficult to measure. My conclusion is that immigration overall has boosted not just the size of the UK's economy, but made us, on average, more prosperous, productive and dynamic – though there is plenty of room for argument, and the nature of both immigration and the domestic economic environment matters as much, if not more, as the number of immigrants.

what do we know about immigration? beyond economics

Economic migration and its impacts on the UK is only part of the picture. In this chapter I move beyond the narrow economic issues to look at some of the other reasons people migrate – as refugees or as irregular migrants. One criticism frequently levelled at economists who discuss immigration is that we are missing the real story, that focusing on the impacts on growth or wages ignores the social changes that result from large inflows of people, so I also briefly examine what the evidence tells us on these topics. Finally, migration does not just affect the society to which people migrate – it also affects the countries they leave.

Refugees

As explained in Chapter 1, large flows of people seeking refuge from war or persecution are nothing new, globally or for the UK. However, since the fall of the Iron Curtain, ethnic persecution and civil wars have resulted in large refugee flows to the EU, including the UK. In 2015, 1.3 million people claimed asylum in the EU, many of whom arrived in dangerous sea voyages from Turkey to Greece or across the Mediterranean to Italy.

Managing these flows has been complicated by the fact that they are often mixed with people whose main motivation for migration is economic, but for whom no appropriate legal route exists, and therefore seek to claim asylum. A large proportion of the 2015 arrivals were Syrians fleeing the continuing civil war, but many others were from sub-Saharan Africa – some from war-torn countries or countries where political or ethnic persecution is rife, but others not.

But these boundaries are not by any means clear, legally, economically or morally. An Afghan man who seeks asylum in the UK, not because he is being individually persecuted, but because his home town is at risk of Taliban attack and there are no economic prospects (at least in part because of UK military intervention), has both political and economic motivations. Furthermore, these pressures are unlikely to diminish; while the Syrian civil war, like the Yugoslav one, will eventually be resolved, other civil and ethnic conflicts are likely in the Middle East and Africa. Demographic pressures and climate change will also emerge.

A full exploration of these issues, and the appropriate political and legal response, is outside the scope of this book. However, it is worth examining the economic implications for the UK. It might seem obvious from an economic perspective that, compared with people who move for work purposes, refugees are likely to represent a significant cost to the host country. By definition, they are not moving to take up or (in the first instance) to seek employment. They will not necessarily have any knowledge of the language or culture and are likely to need state support initially for housing and other services. And they may be traumatised by their experiences, which may make it more difficult for them to enter the labour market.

However, there are also arguments on the other side. In particular, refugees, in contrast to most economic migrants, usually will not have the option to return home or to move to a third country; they may thus be more committed psychologically to their 'new' country and have a greater incentive to learn the language and integrate. Indeed, historical experience, at least in the UK, is actually quite positive. Both the Huguenots and the Jews have been very successful, socially and economically, as, more recently, were the East African Asians (see Appendix A).

It is too soon to know what the longer term outcomes of more recent flows will be. It is often argued that more recent arrivals are less educated, less willing to integrate, and more 'different' (often referring to ethnicity or religion, particularly, in both the United States and European countries, to Muslims). Perhaps – although all this was said about the Jews and the East African Asians at the time. It is true that employment rates for recent refugees are low. What is clear, however, is that refugee outcomes are not determined just by the characteristics of the refugees themselves – the refugee resettlement process and the wider environment in the host country matter at least as much. Outcomes for Somali refugees, for example, are considerably better in the United States than in the UK; in Canada, refugees, often from similar backgrounds to UK refugees, see employment rates rise to close to the national average relatively quickly.

The inefficient and sometimes arbitrary UK asylum process makes matters worse. Pressures on staff to take as hard a line as possible mean claims are often rejected despite strong evidence, or there being little or no prospect of the claimants returning to their country of origin. This means that there are thousands of appeals (a large proportion of which succeed), clogging up the system. The result is that applicants often have to wait for years before reaching a final decision. Meanwhile, refugees are prohibited from working (ostensibly to reduce the incentive for spurious claims), meaning that they are either in severe financial hardship or working irregularly. If they do secure refugee status, giving them entitlement to work, their access to state support is quickly removed. While all of this may save (relatively small) amounts of taxpayer money in the short run, it seems likely that investing in proper support, focused on getting refugees into sustainable work as quickly as possible, would be more economic over the medium to long term.

We should remember, however, that from the broader perspective of geography, combined with the fact that the UK has chosen to remain outside the Schengen system (no border controls between most European countries), means that refugee flows to the UK are relatively small, certainly compared with other EU countries like Germany, Greece and Italy – let alone countries that are closer to major sources of refugees such as Turkey and Jordan. In 2017, there were about 30,000 asylum claims in the UK, equal to less than 0.05% of the UK population. About 5% of asylum claims in Europe were made in the UK, although we have more than 10% of the population.

Illegal and irregular migration

For obvious reasons, we know far less about illegal migration to the UK than about the other topics discussed in this book. Even definitions are not as clear cut as might be thought. Surely anyone who did not arrive legally in this country, or who no longer has permission to remain here, is an 'illegal immigrant'? Yes and no. The Windrush scandal arose because people who had arrived here perfectly legally, and were under no obligation to do anything to prove this to anybody, found that because of a retrospective change in the law they did have such an obligation – and that the Home Office was requiring evidence of their arrival and continuous residence which for many was difficult or impossible to obtain. Such circumstances are not uncommon – people can find that their right to reside here is withdrawn because they or the Home Office lose documents or make relatively trivial mistakes. Equally, such errors can be corrected through reviews, appeals or court cases.

Nor is it always the case that someone who is here under such circumstances has broken the law, or at least not immigration law. Asylum seekers who arrive here via smugglers or with false documentation, may well have broken the law in doing so. But, having claimed asylum they are not 'illegal immigrants' because they are fully entitled, under both UK and international law, to be in the country while their claims are being assessed. For these reasons, it is preferable to refer to irregular, rather than illegal, migrants.

It is also important to remember that, despite the media coverage, only a relatively small proportion of the irregular population, perhaps only 20%, arrived here illegally via the routes that get most publicity, such as being smuggled across the Channel in a lorry. Many or most of those will claim asylum in due course. Far more common are 'overstayers' – those who arrived here perfectly legally, but whose permission to stay here was temporary and has now expired.

So how many irregular migrants are there in the UK? There is absolutely no evidence to support frequent claims in the popular press that there are more than a million. The most recent credible published estimate gave a range, reflecting the uncertainty involved, of 420,000 to 860,000 (of which up to 144,000 are actually children born in the UK, so certainly not what most people would think of as 'immigrants'). But this is now wildly out of date; it was published in 2007, using data from the 2001 census (Gordon et al., 2009).

Since then, both immigration and the number of people coming to the UK temporarily have risen, so the number of potential irregular migrants has too. On the other hand, the number of asylum seekers has fallen considerably from the early 2000s, while many of those from that period who had their claims rejected (or simply not processed) have now been regularised through a number of amnesties. The accession of Bulgaria and Romania will have further reduced numbers. New Home Office data on students suggests that the extent of overstaying was hugely exaggerated. Overall, it seems likely that the numbers have, if anything, fallen. Certainly, estimates of a million or more seem entirely implausible – they would imply that approximately 1 in 7 of the foreign-born population of London were here irregularly.

If a figure of half a million or so adults remains valid, then this is sizable but still well below 1% of the population – much lower than in the United States, where estimates are usually 3–4% of the population. The pervasive labour market impacts of irregular migration that are visible in the United States are also much less apparent in the UK. There clearly are examples of abusive and often illegal exploitation, often related to irregular migrants, ranging from non-payment of the minimum wage right up to human trafficking and modern slavery; but all the available evidence suggests that the numbers involved are small. That is not to minimise the seriousness of these issues, but they do not represent the experiences of the vast majority of irregular migrants, let alone migrants overall. Equally, however, some form of amnesty for irregular migrants – while probably sensible for some categories of people who have been here a long time – is not in itself a panacea, as the irregular population is constantly changing.

The fact that irregular immigration, despite being undesirable and damaging in some respects, is not overall a major social or economic problem does not stop newspapers and politicians using it as a political weapon. Theresa May's 'hostile environment' policy was designed to make it more difficult for people with no right to be here, by preventing them taking jobs, accessing public services, finding a place to live, and so on, so that they would 'self-deport'. This sounded reasonable on its face – why should those who have no entitlement to be here and hence no entitlement to public services be able to access driving licences, the benefits system, education for their children, bank accounts, and so on? But it quickly ran up against the obstacles above. The dividing line between legality and irregularity is blurred, and the fact that someone cannot produce all the documents that might be legally required on demand (often through no fault of their own) does not mean that they are not legally here, still less that they should be denied healthcare or education. In practice, that is exactly what is happening.

It is often argued that we could control irregular migration better if we had complete records of everyone entering and leaving the country.

UK airports and ports saw 135 million arrivals in 2017 (most British and European) and a similar number of departures. If we did record them all, this might help, but only to a certain degree. Most obviously, there are no border controls at all between Ireland and Northern Ireland, and this will remain the case after Brexit since both sides have agreed to maintain the Common Travel Area which allows people to move back and forth across the Irish border with no checks at all. In any case, even if we know that an individual is overstaying their visa, this does not mean that we can find them. Realistically, if the UK wants to control irregular migration, that means a population register linked to a universal identifier, and the controversy over the proposed introduction of ID cards in the mid-2000s suggests we are not ready for that.

Meanwhile, the immediate challenge facing the system is the 3.5 million EU citizens currently resident here. They have been offered the opportunity to acquire 'settled status' – giving them the right to permanent residence – and a new system has now been introduced to allow them to apply. It is likely that most will do so and will therefore have their future residency status guaranteed. But inevitably when dealing with such large numbers of people, there will be errors, omissions, and an unknown number who simply will not apply, and will therefore, at some point, become irregular. If this is tens of thousands, it may be manageable; if it is hundreds of thousands, the UK's irregular migration problem will suddenly become much more complex.

Integration and social cohesion

In 1978, as leader of the Opposition, Margaret Thatcher said, 'People are really rather afraid that this country might be swamped by people with a different culture' (Thatcher, 1978). More recently and in less emotive language, but with similar undertones, the then Home Secretary Theresa May argued, 'When immigration is too high, when the pace of change is too fast, it's impossible to build a cohesive society' (BBC News, 2015).

It is easy for those on the liberal side of the debate to dismiss such sentiments simply as code words for racism – and sometimes they are – but most public opinion research suggests that they are shared by the majority of the population in some form. Equally, however, this does not mean that we cannot examine the evidence, or otherwise, that underlies them.

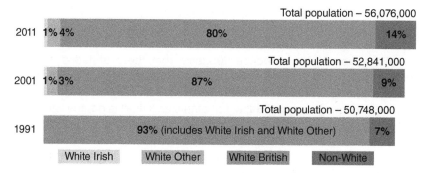

Figure 4.1 Growth of ethnic diversity in England & Wales, 1991–2001–2011

Source: Jivraj (2012)

Immigration on a sufficient scale does, quite literally, change the nature of a country's population – well over a third of babies born in the UK in 2017 had at least one parent who was born abroad. The ethnic character of the country has already changed considerably (see Figure 4.1) and will do so even further over the next few decades, even if immigration slows down considerably. The UK is visibly and recognisably a multi-ethnic society in a way that it was not when I was a child.

Whether this is a good or bad thing, or indeed neither, depends on your perspective. Twitter is full of lunatics who talk about 'race replacement' or 'white genocide'. But there are more respectable versions of essentially the same argument to be found among intellectuals or the mainstream press, often advanced by those who would like to see immigration sharply reduced or eliminated. The majority of London's population is no longer 'white British', but a substantial majority of us were born here, and an even larger majority identify as British (white, black, Asian or mixed) and have British citizenship. Nevertheless, the eminent economist Sir Paul Collier, cited these statistics to claim that the 'indigenous British' (meaning white British, but not black, Asian or indeed mixed-race people, even if born here) had become a 'minority in their own capital'. Meanwhile, Douglas Murray, a contributor to *The Spectator* and *The Daily Telegraph* who argues for reducing or eliminating Muslim immigration into Europe, said that the same figures mean that London has become a 'foreign country'.

So the view that you have to be white to be 'really' British, and that black or Asian Britons are still somehow alien and threatening, remains prevalent, even if largely hidden, in some elite circles.

Nevertheless, the evidence suggests that these attitudes and the broader conception of Britishness as being fundamentally related to ethnicity, skin colour or religion are not shared by the majority. Rather, there is a much larger group who think that ethnicity in itself is not the issue, but rather how people of different ethnicities and backgrounds interact with each other (Ballinger, 2018). This discussion often generates more heat than light. It has become commonplace over the last decade for politicians and commentators in the UK to claim that 'multiculturalism has failed', yet few of those who do so could present a coherent definition of the term or explain in what sense it has been tried in the UK, let alone evidence that it has 'failed'. I do not intend to discuss here the complex issues surrounding integration, assimilation and multiculturalism, but rather to examine what the evidence tells us.

The first, and perhaps most important, fact is that as the UK has become less ethnically homogeneous, racist attitudes have become significantly less prevalent. While the proportion of people who say that they share some racist sentiments has not reduced much in the last two decades, that in itself reflects shifting norms: responses to more 'objective' questions like 'would you mind if a close family member married someone of another ethnic group?' show a very clear shift (Kelley et al., 2017). This is reflected in both individual experience and what is acceptable in public and popular discourse; the sort of casual racism that was common in the playground and in the popular (and sometimes even serious) press when I was a child would simply not be tolerated today.

This does not mean that racism, both at an individual and at a structural level, does not remain a serious issue. And some forms of racism, notably Islamophobia, are both prevalent and, in some circles, respectable. Nevertheless, overall, the UK is a recognisably functional multi-ethnic society in a way that it was not in the 1980s.

Similarly, while ethnic inequalities in employment, incomes and poverty remain persistent and large, they have generally reduced over time. This is particularly the case for education, where some ethnic minority groups outperform whites, and, more importantly, the variation within groups is vastly greater than the differences between them, suggesting that most of the issues with the education system are not related to ethnicity.

Attitudes and values are harder to measure. One concern that is frequently raised is that immigration and the ethnic diversity that has accompanied it have undermined the UK's national identity. It is very hard to see any evidence for this in the data; across all ethnic groups, the vast majority of UK residents feel strongly that they 'belong to Britain' (Press Association, 2012) and identify strongly either as British or as English/ Welsh/Scottish, with non-white ethnic groups rather more likely to iden- tify as British (and whites as English/Welsh/Scottish). There has been no decrease in this tendency over time. Equally, most British people, including white British, reject the so-called 'Tebbit cricket test' (named after a Conservative Cabinet Minister in the 1980s who argued that Britons of an immigrant background could not be considered fully British unless they supported the British (or English!) team against that of the country from which their family originated). Now, however, it is generally accepted that one can be fully British while retaining a separate cultural or religious identity.

There are clear differences in some attitudes between groups. In particular, Muslims, on average, have considerably more conservative attitudes on some social issues (homosexuality, equal marriage, etc.) and attach much more importance to religion than those of other faiths (let alone those of none) (Ipsos MORI, 2018). However, these attitudes are not particularly uncommon among older white Britons – indeed, they were mainstream in the main political parties 20 years ago – and they appear to be diminishing among younger Muslims.

But equality and even tolerance are possible without integration. Are we a more integrated society, in the sense of living, working, socialising together? The former head of the Equality and Human Rights Commission, Trevor Phillips, famously claimed in 2005 that the UK was 'sleepwalking to segregation' (Phillips, 2005), while in 2016 the government published a report that described some, mostly Muslim, communities as living 'isolated, separate lives' (Casey, 2016).

In fact, the evidence for this is weak. Immigrants do tend to locate in areas where others of the same community also live when they first arrive in a country, for obvious reasons. And this can help rather than hinder integration if it makes it easier for them to get jobs. The UK is full of rec- ognisably distinct areas where certain ethnic groups have concentrated, from Sikhs in Southall or Pakistanis in Bradford to, less obviously, Koreans in New Malden. But residential segregation – how likely people are to live in areas dominated by the same ethnic group – has decreased, not increased, over time, although the pace of change is slow (Catney, 2013). It is worth remembering that for obvious and simple arithmetic reasons, the group most likely to be segregated, in the sense of not having friends or neighbours from different ethnic groups, not working with or attending school with other ethnic groups, is white British. People from ethnic minority groups are much less likely to be in this position.

Indeed, while immigration has increased hugely over the last two decades, it has also become far more diverse, so there are far more areas where no single ethnic group is in an overwhelming majority. For example, areas like Tower Hamlets and Newham in East London, where the majority of people are foreign born, are not dominated by any specific group (Tower Hamlets is about a third white British, a third Bangladeshi British and a third other groups). Again, this is not to deny that there are areas where ethnic segregation has persisted, in particular between Pakistani and white communities in some medium-sized towns and cities in the north of England. Here there are a complex set of issues at work, in particular relating to the combination of immigration, culture, race/racism and economic decline. Nevertheless, overall, the picture remains one of slow but relatively steady decline in segregation.

And while it is obviously difficult to measure integration at a personal level, again the picture appears to be broadly positive. Interracial relationships have become increasingly common and the social acceptance of such relationships has become the norm (indeed the fastest growing 'ethnic group' in the UK, by some margin, is 'mixed race'), although there are considerable differences between ethnic groups, reflecting both cultural factors and the different circumstances in which they arrived in the UK (Platt, 2009).

But, despite all this, does immigration diminish the quality of life for people who are already residents, as Theresa May argued, simply because of the 'pace of change'? The Office for National Statistics now publishes survey evidence on 'subjective well-being', or life satisfaction (sometimes described simply as 'happiness') in the UK. Research finds that the impact of immigration on life satisfaction at a local level is actually positive, although quite small (Giulietti and Yan, 2018). Nor is there any evidence that this is because people who do not like immigration move away from high-immigration areas (so-called 'white flight'). So whatever people may say to opinion polls about immigration at a national level, there is no evidence that having lots of immigrants reduces quality of life locally.

Crime

One particularly sensitive area in this respect is crime: the belief that immigration increases crime is widespread in developed countries, although such beliefs seem to have little correlation with the actual prevalence of crime or number of immigrants. It is plausible to think that immigrants might be more likely to commit crimes if they are poorer, or have fewer savings or other resources to fall back on if they experience hard times. Irregular migrants may be excluded from the labour market, which obviously makes it more likely that they will seek other ways, not necessarily legal, to make money. Immigrants are also more likely to live in cities and in relatively poor areas, where crime levels overall are typically higher. So from the point of view of the general public it may seem logical to associate immigration and crime. However, equally, immigrants may face greater penalties, including deportation, if they engage in criminal activities.

Overall, most research finds little or no connection between immigration and crime. In the United States, despite Trump's rhetoric, immigrants – both legal and illegal – seem to be somewhat less likely to commit crimes (excluding specifically immigration-related ones) than native-born Americans (Nowrasteh, 2018). In the UK, foreign nationals are about 12% of the prison population, very similar to their share of the adult population. More detailed research suggests that increases in the number of refugees and asylum seekers did lead to a slight increase in property crime – presumably because many were forbidden from working and had access to little or no other opportunities to support themselves – while more recent economic migration led to a slight decrease (Bell et al., 2013). There was no relationship with violent crime.

So, overall, any impacts on crime rates appear to be quite small, and as with unemployment the big picture is very clear: crime has fallen sharply in the UK over the last two decades just as the immigrant population began to grow rapidly. Even after recent rises, London's murder rate remains far below the levels of the early 1990s.

Nevertheless, there clearly is an association between immigration and some forms of crime. In particular, organised crime relies on business relationships maintained by bonds of trust and non-legal sanctions for 'cheating'. This in turn requires close-knit social networks. Since recent immigrant communities often have such networks – and may also have connections to countries of origin which facilitate certain types of crime like smuggling – it is no surprise that in many countries organised crime is based on ethnically defined networks. Recently in the UK, there has been considerable publicity around the sexual abuse of young girls, often by men of Pakistani origin, in some communities, again centred around loosely organised social networks.

Conclusion

The critics of the liberal stance are right in one respect. It is reasonably clear that while migration has economic costs and benefits, the net impacts are broadly positive. But by contrast, it is impossible simply to add up all the evidence on social impacts and come to a similarly clear-cut conclusion, both because those impacts are more diverse and harder to measure and because some of them are largely or wholly subjective. But equally we do have some evidence, both quantitative and qualitative, and it does suggest that some of the rhetoric is, at the very least, grossly exaggerated. There is very little to substantiate the claim that the UK is becoming more segregated or more divided on ethnic grounds, or that groups are choosing to form self-perpetuating enclaves, physical, social or attitudinal. From my perspective, it suggests that the glass is (at least) half-full, rather than half-empty.

what should we do about immigration?

Immigration policy in an age of populism

It should be apparent from the previous chapters that the evidence in my view – from both the UK and elsewhere – suggests that the benefits of immigration, overall, are substantial while the costs are often illusory or exaggerated. But 'what we should do' about immigration policy is a political question just as much, if not more, as an economic one, and is inevitably framed by the context. Those of us seeking to help frame policy need to do so in the context of Trump, Brexit and the rise of populism across much of Europe. So in this chapter I consider how things might develop from where we are now.

First, that means understanding why we are where we are, politically. If the economic benefits of immigration are well established and for the most part broadly spread, what explains the recent political backlash across much of the developed world? It seems intuitive that there must be a connection between the election of Trump, the UK's vote to leave the EU and the rise of far-right populists in much of Continental Europe, from France and Italy to Hungary and Poland.

But while anti-immigrant rhetoric and sentiment is a common theme, the circumstances of individual countries are very different. In the United States, Trump focused on irregular migration from Mexico and Central America and their supposed impacts on crime and security. In the UK, the ostensible focus of the Brexit campaign was on free movement within the EU, predominantly of white East Europeans – although the potential for future migration from Turkey and other countries further east was also a strong theme. In West European countries like Sweden, Germany, France and Italy, already existing right-wing populists were boosted by public reaction to refugee and migrant flows from Syria and Africa. In Poland and Hungary, despite the fact that immigrant flows are extremely small, parties in power have successfully appealed to nationalist sentiments with a focus specifically on the threat of Muslim immigration overrunning 'Christian' Europe.

Neither economics nor politics can, in themselves, provide a common thread linking these disparate phenomena. Economic trends flowing from globalisation clearly are relevant; the electoral strength of Trump, Brexit and the French far-right in areas that were most affected by deindustrialisation in the 1980s and 1990s is well established. But the direct link with immigration is far from clear.

There is no question that those with negative attitudes towards immigration are more likely to vote for right-wing populists, but those attitudes are also strongly correlated with authoritarian and socially conservative views across the board. There are also major differences across countries, with racist attitudes towards ethnic minorities being both stronger and a better predictor of voting patterns in some countries than others. Overall, the patterns of causation between economic conditions, attitudes towards immigration and political outcomes are complex and multi-dimensional.

Immigration and the Brexit vote

The above is certainly true of the UK's vote to leave the EU. While anti-EU feeling in the UK has deep roots, before the late 2000s the EU and immigration were largely separate issues in UK politics. In the 1975 referendum on EU membership, immigration was not a significant issue at all, and voters with more negative attitudes towards immigration were no more likely to vote to leave. But to the extent that the 2016 Brexit vote was a vote for, or more specifically against, anything, it was a vote against free movement of workers within the EU. The slogan 'Vote Leave, Take Control', summed up the entire Leave campaign, whether referring to the fictional £350 million per week that the UK 'sends to Brussels' or to our supposed ability speedily to conclude advantageous free trade deals with third countries once freed from the dead hand of EU control of UK trade policy.

However, it was particularly effective and resonant with respect to immigration policy and border control because it contained a very large element of truth: free movement of workers is one of the foundational 'four freedoms' of the EU and as long as it remains a member, the UK is obliged to respect this central obligation. So the Remain campaign found it extremely difficult to counter the simple argument that the only way for the UK to 'control' immigration was to leave.

Negative attitudes to immigration and in particular free movement within the EU are very strongly associated with opposition to UK membership. Post-referendum polling by Lord Ashcroft found that approximately 80% of those who thought that immigration was mostly a force for good voted to Remain, while a similar proportion of those who thought of it as a force for ill voted to Leave.

The evidence is less clear as to whether immigration, either from within the EU or more generally, was the key driving factor in the vote to leave. Certainly it was not the case that, overall, areas where there were higher levels of immigration voted Leave (London was both the most pro-Remain region of England and the region with by far the highest proportion of immigrants). However, some analyses suggested that areas which had experienced large recent migrant flows (at least on a proportional basis) were more likely to vote Leave – and recent EU migration was undoubtedly a factor in some specific areas, such as Boston in Lincolnshire, which saw the highest Leave vote in the country (Goodwin and Milazzo, 2017).

Alternative explanations also exist that focus more directly on economic factors, ranging from the long-term impacts of deindustrialisation to the impact of more recent cuts to public services and welfare benefits. Clearly monocausal explanations are insufficient. But to any casual observer of the national-level campaign, it is clear that – outside London at least – perceptions of the impact of migration were indeed a key factor in driving the Leave vote, even if that vote was not itself strongest in areas of very high immigration. It is therefore not surprising that immigration – and what Brexit will mean for UK immigration policy – is equally central to the post-referendum debate.

The government's proposals

At the time of writing, it is still unclear what exactly Brexit will look like and indeed if it will happen at all. But, assuming it does proceed broadly along the lines planned by the government, Brexit and the end of free movement will be the biggest shakeup of the UK immigration system for at least two decades. Although the current Withdrawal Agreement, which governs the terms of the UK's 'divorce' from the EU, contains extensive provisions relating to EU citizens currently resident in the UK (and British residents elsewhere in the EU), it does not contain any provisions directly relating to future UK immigration policy, though it does confirm that the Common Travel Area between the UK and Ireland will continue, meaning that the prospect of the UK fully 'controlling its borders' with respect to the movement of people remains as far away as ever.

However, the Political Declaration, which sets out the framework for the future relationship between the UK and the EU, states clearly that the UK will end free movement of people. It also refers to short-term business visits and visas. The UK (in the so-called Chequers White Paper) and the EU27 have previously referred to 'ambitious provisions' on labour mobility, so there is no reason at this stage to think this means anything more ambitious than those contained in the existing Canada–EU trade deal, which have little or no impact on immigration policy.

This suggests that, if the Withdrawal Agreement is passed, free movement of people with the EU will come to an end and the UK will largely be free to set its own immigration policy after the end of the transition period in 2021 or 2022, with relatively little constraint from any agreements with the EU. What policy would be adopted, and what would the economic impacts be?

The Migration Advisory Committee (MAC), in its report on the impact of EEA migration published in September 2018 (Migration Advisory Committee, 2018), made a number of recommendations on post-Brexit immigration policy. The government responded positively to the MAC report and on 19 December 2018 published a White Paper on future immigration policy (Home Office, 2018). The White Paper incorporates the key recommendations from the MAC:

a   Unless a future trade agreement with the EU provides otherwise, there should be no 'European preference' for EU or EEA citizens seeking to move to the UK for work purposes after Brexit. In other words, after the end of free movement, there should be no intermediate position where EU or EEA citizens still find it easier to move to the UK than non-EU ones.

b EU/EEA citizens would therefore have to apply for permission to live and work in the UK in the same way as non-EU citizens do at present. In practice, for most of those seeking to move here to work this will mean applying for a Tier 2 ('skilled worker') visa, which requires the applicant to satisfy a number of criteria (relating, depending on the job, to salary, occupation, skill level and the non-availability of workers from within the UK). Various fees and charges are also payable.

c The MAC recommended that the existing salary threshold of £30,000 for Tier 2 visas should be maintained. However, while the White Paper takes this as the starting point, it is explicitly subject to consultation, and businesses (and, privately, some Cabinet Ministers) have argued for a lower threshold.

d The White Paper also recommended that the Tier 2 visa route be simplified and liberalised in a number of respects, and the White Paper broadly accepts these recommendations. In particular, it recommended that the current 'cap' on the number of Tier 2 visas should be removed, that the Resident Labour Market Test (RLMT) should be abolished and that the minimum skill level required should be reduced (so that broadly jobs requiring A-level skills or above would qualify, as long as the salary threshold was met). Nevertheless, applying for a Tier 2 visa would still involve considerable costs to both employers and migrants and the completion of numerous administrative tasks.

e The Shortage Occupation List (SOL), which specifies jobs for which a Tier 2 visa may be issued relatively easily even if other criteria (in particular the salary threshold) are not met, would remain and the White Paper specifically raises the possibility of extending the current arrangements for Scotland, which has its own SOL, to Wales. It is unclear how the SOL would in practice operate under the new system. If the other changes are implemented – the abolition of the cap, the RLMT and the reduction in the minimum skill level – the SOL would arguably be largely redundant except with respect to the salary threshold. It is unclear whether the MAC would consider extending the SOL to occupations such as, for example, social care workers, where salaries and required skill/qualification levels would be below the new thresholds.

f   The White Paper also proposes the introduction of a temporary work visa for migrants earning less than the salary cap coming from 'low-risk' countries (i.e. those whose nationals are viewed as unlikely to overstay). This would be valid for a year and on expiry the holder would have to leave the UK for at least a year. The White Paper has very little detail on how this would operate in practice.

What would this mean in practice for different groups of potential immigrants? For these purposes, we can divide work-related migrants into four categories, and describe in broad terms how they will be affected:

a   EU migrants earning less than £30,000 (assuming that this is indeed the eventual threshold). These currently benefit from free movement. Under the proposed system, they would not be able to obtain a Tier 2 visa (of course, some may be able to move to the UK through other routes which allow work, for example family/spouse visas). They would also be eligible for the new temporary visa. This would be the group most directly affected.

b   EU migrants earning more than £30,000. Again, these benefit from free movement. In future, they would in most cases in principle be able to secure a work visa. However, they would face very significant new barriers; they would have to have a job offer, they or their employers would need to pay various fees and charges, and the current bureaucratic process is extremely burdensome. Moreover, as well as these costs, there are other reasons why it is less attractive to be resident in the UK on a Tier 2 visa than via freedom of movement: the former offer has fewer rights, in particular with respect to other family members and access to public services and welfare, and also faces additional barriers (in particular, a further, higher, salary threshold, currently £35,000) should the migrants seek to apply for permanent settlement. So this group will face a considerably more restrictive migration regime, new financial disincentives and opportunity costs, and a less attractive status in the UK once here.

c   Non-EU migrants earning less than £30,000. This group cannot, by and large, migrate for work purposes to the UK under the current regime. Under the new regime some, from 'low-risk' countries, might be able apply for the new temporary work visa. Beyond this, there will be no significant direct effects.

d   Non-EU migrants earning more than £30,000. As set out above, the White Paper sets out a number of measures that will have the effect of liberalising migration for this group. In particular, the removal of the current quota of 20,700 for Tier 2 visas will mean that there is no longer an upper limit on numbers (although this limit has only been binding for limited periods over the last seven years) while the reduction in the minimum skill level will also have an impact. The White Paper also sets out measures to streamline and simplify the system; in principle, this could have a significant impact, but this will obviously depend on how it is implemented.

So the UK would move to a system where economic migration, at least, was open only to immigrants with a job offer that exceeded the £30,000 threshold, perhaps with some schemes to cover specific 'shortage occupations'. On one level, this would represent a move towards a more 'normal' system – it is not, conceptually, very different from that used by the United States, Canada, Australia or New Zealand or other advanced economies that are not part of the EU Single Market and hence of the EU's free movement area. But precisely because it has been part of the free movement zone for so long, the UK's immigration system and labour market are very different; the adjustment process is likely to be difficult and prolonged.

Take the care sector, where many, including the MAC, argue that the real problem driving recruitment and retention of staff is sustained government underfunding. It is hard to argue with that. But, after Brexit, is the government really going to break the habit of at least two decades and fund the sector properly? Will it just let services get worse and worse, or will it introduce a special scheme, despite the MAC recommendation that it do no such thing? In practice, when the potential impact of these proposals becomes apparent, some modifications are likely.

There are also broader issues. The argument made for a system like this is that it would ensure that future economic migration was only of the 'skilled' workers that the UK needs. In fact, these proposals would exclude not just low-skilled workers but almost everyone earning under £30,000, well above average full-time earnings. So this would not just hit fruit-pickers and baristas but butchers, primary school teachers, radiographers, and so on. None of these, and many others, are jobs that can be done without training or qualifications. So, while making it easier for skilled workers to come here from outside the EU makes sense, it may get much harder to fill a lot of jobs that the UK economy needs.

Moreover, as set out earlier, the case for maintaining some form of free movement with the EU even after Brexit is considerably stronger than the report suggests. It is true that the current system, where it is much easier for EU migrants to come here than non-EU ones, is far less 'selective' for the former than the latter. But despite this, EU migrants still have higher employment rates and make a larger fiscal contribution than either people born here or migrants from elsewhere. This suggests that free movement, 'uncontrolled' as it is, is not working out too badly for the UK.

Of course, it is always possible in principle to improve things even more by being more 'selective'. But selection has to be applied in practice not by a perfect system but by bureaucrats in Whitehall. There is little evidence that a government-planned and regulated approach will in fact outperform the current largely market-driven system of free movement. Indeed, even the government's own estimates of the impact of the proposed changes are that they will reduce UK GDP and UK GDP per capita – in other words, they would make the UK less prosperous and less productive, albeit those impacts will probably be smaller than the broader impacts of Brexit.

The proposals for a 'temporary work visa' seem even harder to justify. It is questionable whether an explicitly temporary route would be attractive to either employers or workers in skilled or semi-skilled jobs, for example in manufacturing (where at least some on-the-job training is required and productivity is likely to rise with job tenure) or in other occupations like social care. But more broadly, there are considerable potential downsides to what would effectively be a 'guest worker' route, where migrants would have fewer rights and the potential for abuse by unscrupulous employers would be correspondingly greater. To the extent that concerns about the impacts of immigration are related to the potential for exploitation or abuse; 'undercutting' of native workers; or excessive population 'churn' and the associated social costs, this proposal would increase rather than reduce the risks.

More broadly, the UK government has not yet made the big decisions. The Cabinet, Conservative Party and country more widely (especially those who voted for Brexit) are divided. Some recognise that – after Brexit, more than ever – the economy needs a relatively liberal immigration system, particularly if we are going to make a reality of 'global Britain'. The evidence backs them up and suggests that if free movement is indeed to end, this logically means a substantial liberalisation of the rest of the system, rebalancing it in favour of non-EU migrants – unless we want to do still further damage to the economy and public finances. This view is increasingly shared by the UK public, which in recent years has become significantly more positive about the impact of immigration. Much remains to play for.

A better way?

So what would a more positive strategy look like? Theresa May, both as Home Secretary and as Prime Minister, made reducing immigration the primary objective of policy, even to the point of claiming that a fall in the number of international students coming to the UK was a success. Whatever happens to Brexit, we need to move beyond that if the UK is to remain a successful, open economy. The first priority should be simply to make clear that immigration, like trade, is indeed central to making the UK open for business and hence to our growth strategy.

The next step would be then to take the opportunity of Brexit and to examine each aspect of immigration policy – not just with regards to people coming here to work, but students, family members, refugees, and so on – with a view towards reorienting them towards the needs of the economy and society as a whole, instead of the current obsession with 'control'.

The government's current approach seems to be to apply a modified version of the current system for non-EU workers to EU citizens who currently benefit from freedom of movement. This may look like the line of least resistance from a bureaucratic perspective, but risks missing the bigger picture. There are many sensible changes, major and minor, that are required. But in my view, more important than specific policy changes is a change of attitude and mindset on the part of government and policy makers. If we want to be serious about growth, we will need to be positive about migration.

So, for example, the current attitude of the UK government towards foreign students is that they are, in principle, welcome so long as they leave when they have finished their studies, so not becoming permanent immigrants. But, from both an economic and a social point of view, students who do choose to remain are likely to be highly beneficial to the UK. By definition, they are relatively highly skilled and well educated. Their English is likely to be good, they will have already had considerable experience of living in the UK and at least to some extent they may be integrated into UK society. Anyone who, after a few years of studying here, positively wants to stay here for good is probably going to be precisely the type of immigrant we want. So, while there will always have to be rules, encouraging and facilitating international students to remain here after graduation is a relatively easy win in immigration policy terms. Other countries, like the United States and Australia, currently do a better job of this than we do.

Another unnecessary own goal is the UK's current policies on permanent settlement. Even if you come here as a skilled worker and remain in your job for five years, if after that time you do not pass a further – higher – salary threshold, you can be kicked out, even if you have successfully integrated into both the UK labour market and broader society. This particularly affects people working in skilled occupations in the public sector, such as teachers and nurses. Not only is it damaging economically, but from a broader social perspective, forcing people who have lived here happily enough for several years to leave is hardly conducive to integration.

But, as I have repeatedly emphasised, it is not just or perhaps even mainly about economics. Again, Brexit offers a window of opportunity. Public concern about immigration has fallen sharply since the Brexit vote and public attitudes towards the impacts of immigration are more positive than they have been for many years. Politicians could choose this moment to make the case for liberal policy not just on economic grounds, but also to address some of the wider issues. This would include both defences of the rights of immigrants themselves (e.g. of EU citizens currently resident in the UK, of the UK-born children of immigrants who are denied rights to UK citizenship, of UK citizens who marry people from abroad, and so on). It would also include a more positive approach to the impacts of immigration on communities and services at a local level – by promoting integration and ensuring funding was channelled to areas where there are genuine pressures resulting from population growth.

Integration is about much more than money and the UK's record to date is far more positive than some public debate suggests. Recently, some academics have argued that negative public attitudes towards immigration relate primarily to fears about its impact on identity and culture more than economics, and this is certainly consistent with much of the data presented above (Eatwell and Goodwin, 2018).

But I do not believe that it is credible to argue that restricting immigration to certain, supposedly more culturally acceptable groups will somehow be good for integration. The idea, advanced by the author Douglas Murray (Murray, 2017), that we should drastically reduce Muslim immigration because of its 'alien' and 'colonising' nature, is not just ahistorical and offensive to many; it would also be deeply divisive in a country where there are already more than 2.5 million Muslim residents. Treating millions of our fellow citizens as inferior is not going to do much for social cohesion.

A similar argument is offered by Eric Kaufmann, a political scientist, who suggests that we should give preferences in immigration policy to people from ethnic or cultural backgrounds which are, by some metric, easier to assimilate (Kaufmann, 2018). He suggests an illustrative ranking with Anglo-Canadians at the top, followed by Poles and Afro-Carribbeans, with Hasidic Jews bringing up the rear. Extra points would be awarded to those who married white people. Again, the idea that creating a racial hierarchy for the purposes of immigration policy will promote ethnic harmony seems misplaced.

In fact, as the Brexit referendum and subsequent events have shown, it is hard to see that simply reducing immigration will do much to allay concerns about identity and culture, which flow more from domestic social change than from ethnic change per se. The UK's internal tensions flow more from geography and class than ethnicity or migrant origin. While, as noted above, authors like Murray and Collier think London now has too many people who are not white, it is London's broader economic and cultural dominance that is more fundamental. Solving some of these wider issues – the relative decline of certain formerly industrialised areas and coastal towns, the underfunding of public services over the last decade, 'precarity' in large segments of the labour market – would go a very long way towards building or rebuilding a sense of shared national identity and in turn addressing broader concerns. If most of us believed our government and politicians when they said that 'we're all in it together', there would be far fewer concerns about immigration or integration.

The broader debate

But leaving the immediate UK debate to one side, let's step back for a minute. There seems little doubt that immigration will remain a central economic and political issue across Europe and the rest of the developed world for the foreseeable future. Driven both by 'supply' (demographic pressures in many developing countries and perhaps climate change) and 'demand' (demography again, with population ageing and below replacement-level fertility rates in most developed countries), the number of people seeking to move countries – whether economic migration, refugee flows, or a mix – is likely to continue to grow. What approach should the UK and other advanced economies adopt?

From the global perspective, the arguments for a more liberal approach are very strong. My discussion so far has focused on the impacts of immigrants on the society in which they arrive – on wages, jobs and public services – as this affects those of us who are already resident. But immigrants are people too. Unsurprisingly, from an economic perspective, those who gain most at an individual level from immigration are immigrants themselves, since making such gains is precisely the reason they moved countries in the first place – whether in the positive sense of moving for a better job, a higher salary, or better prospects for their family, or the negative one of escaping unemployment, war or persecution. Such gains can be very large. Even within Europe, wage differentials (for the same worker) can easily be two or three to one, while for people from some developing countries the ratio can be much higher. For example, one estimate is that the same person could earn eight times as much in the United States as they would in Haiti.

This in turn means that the potential gains to global welfare from a more liberal policy are potentially huge. At one extreme, some argue that both theory and evidence are so clear that economists should argue for ending all restrictions on migration – an open borders policy. The gains from such a policy could, with not implausible assumptions, amount to a doubling of world GDP, with even larger welfare gains to those who currently live in poorer countries. Others, often lawyers or political philosophers, make the same argument from a rights-based or libertarian perspective (as opposed to the utilitarian or consequentialist perspective generally assumed, implicitly, by economists). In my view, whatever the principled arguments, this is not an argument economists can reasonably hope to win in the foreseeable future in developed countries.

On the other hand, there are also economists who argue that right-wing populism represents a backlash against globalisation, in part justified by objective economic impacts, even if its political manifestation is often deeply unpleasant; and that economists, like me, who claim that those impacts are, at least when it comes to immigration, relatively minor, are wilfully ignoring the negative political consequences. As the leading economist and nuanced critic of globalisation, Dani Rodrik, puts it:

As an emerging new establishment consensus grudgingly concedes, globalization accentuates class divisions between those who have the skills and resources to take advantage of global markets and those who don't ... immigration has overshadowed other globalization 'shocks.' The perceived threat of mass inflows of migrants and refugees from poor countries with very different cultural traditions aggravates identity cleavages that far-right politicians are exceptionally well placed to exploit. (Rodrik, 2016)

From this perspective, the answer is to concentrate on improving domestic policies while accommodating the political pressure to reduce immigration, as well as restraining other aspects of globalisation. While this perspective may appear attractive to politicians who find it increasingly difficult to sustain a broadly 'liberal' approach, I do not think that is likely to be a successful strategy. There is little or no evidence that retreating from support for relatively liberal immigration policies – as opposed to trying to explain the benefits and to address directly any genuine negative impacts, as I suggest above for the UK – will, over the long run, either improve actual outcomes for those most vulnerable to the lure of right-wing populism, or improve public perceptions of the impact of immigration. To the extent that we have positive examples of countries that have combined relatively open policies with public consent, they are those like Ireland, Canada and Spain that have followed the latter approach. Immigration is a rare example of a topic where the evidence is reasonably clear, and economists and other social scientists across the political spectrum broadly agree. Those of us who would like to see economic and social policies that reflect reality rather than prejudice should stand our ground.

This may seem hopelessly naive in the age of Trump and Orbán. But what is the alternative? The pressures – economic, social and geopolitical, from demographics to climate change – will not go away. Building walls – in metaphorical terms, in policy terms, or in concrete or steel – will neither eliminate these pressures nor appease or disempower populists, precisely because immigration will nevertheless continue, in one way or another. Trying both to realise the benefits and to manage the politics will be messy – but the alternatives are far, far worse.

6

conclusion

Writing a book that combines recent history, the latest economic research, contemporary politics and speculation about what can and what should happen next inevitably means that I have been aiming at a moving target. The recent sharp rise in immigration to the UK began in 1997, but we do not know when, if and how it will end and whether Brexit will be a turning point or merely a punctuation mark.

But despite this we have learnt a lot over the last two decades. As I have tried to explain, we can be broadly confident that immigration has been a net plus for the UK economy, however it is measured. Immigrants do not take our jobs, nor do they make us poorer. Fears about the wider impact of immigration – on public services, crime or 'cohesion' – are over-stated. The UK has coped with the challenges of integrating large numbers of migrants reasonably well, and not just people coming here to work, but refugees and others.

Nevertheless, the political backlash against rising immigration has been severe. This is by no means a new phenomenon, but it has had far-reaching implications. While immigration did not in itself 'cause' Brexit and the UK's current slow-motion political crisis, it is difficult to imagine that the UK would have voted to leave the EU without it. This also has parallels elsewhere, in the United States and in Continental Europe.

Perhaps most worryingly, the backlash against immigration has both been exacerbated by and in turn worsened a general sense of alienation among large sections of the UK population. This in part was driven by economics, made worse by austerity, but perhaps even more so by cultural concerns, in turn driven by geography, class and age. This is not just or even mainly about immigration, but it makes it far more difficult for politicians to formulate or implement sensible immigration policies.

But I remain optimistic. Partly that is because I still believe that, despite everything – xenophobic newspapers, cynical politicians and 'respectable' intellectuals and commentators who are quite happy to legitimise racism – the experience of the last two decades has been hugely positive overall, both for the UK and for the immigrants who have made the UK their home. Whatever your views on Brexit and the Brexit process, I do not share the view that the vote to leave was in itself inherently xenophobic.

Indeed, despite all the negative factors listed above, public attitudes to immigration in the UK are at their most positive in decades. There is a window of opportunity to reset not just immigration policy but our broader perspective. This will take a degree of courage and initiative, not just from politicians but from the rest of us. It will be contested, messy and imperfect, just as in every previous historical episode. Nevertheless, I am hopeful that if I come to revise this book in 5 or 10 years from now, I will still be able to paint a positive picture.

appendices

appendix A:
the east african asians

Trade links between the east coast of Africa and the west coast of India, in particularly Gujarat, date back millennia. However, the establishment of settled communities of Indians in East Africa began at the end of the nineteenth century, as a direct result of the incorporation of East Africa into the British Empire. By the time of decolonisation and independence, the Asian communities in Uganda, Kenya, Tanzania and Malawi numbered several hundred thousand.

Colonial policies ensured that they occupied a relatively privileged position economically, with a dominant position in finance and trade (although by no means were all particularly rich: many were small shopkeepers and artisans). At the same time, they were almost entirely segregated, residentially and culturally, from the African majority. Unsurprisingly, this was a recipe for economic and racial tension. The newly independent states pursued policies of 'Africanisation' and Asian communities were both an obvious target for such policies and easy scapegoats when they failed to deliver quick results.

Most East African Asians had the right to enter the UK under the Commonwealth Immigration Act and a steady exodus became a mass outflow in 1967, in response to discriminatory legislation. The UK government responded with legislation designed to exclude Kenyan Asians. However, when President Amin, in August 1972, announced the wholesale expulsion of all Asians from Uganda, the UK reversed its policy and allowed entry, despite considerable domestic opposition. The then UK Prime Minister, Ted Heath, said:

> [The British people] have refused to be scared into supporting the attitude of meanness and bad faith towards the [Ugandan Asian] refugees. They have responded in accordance with our traditions of honouring our obligations and holding out a friendly hand to people in danger and distress.

Estimates vary, but it seems likely that over the period from the early 1960s to the mid-1970s at least 150,000–200,000 East African Asians moved to the UK. Most of the new arrivals settled in areas where there were already existing Gujarati communities, in particular Leicester and parts of north-west London.

The arrival of these Asians in the UK coincided with perhaps the most bitter domestic debate on race and immigration in the UK in the post-war period. Enoch Powell's 'Rivers of Blood' speech in 1968, opposing the Race Relations Act and defending the right to discriminate against non-white Britons, raised racial tensions. There was considerable pressure on the government to reject any responsibility for the Ugandan Asians. Powell said that 'their so-called British passports do not entitle them to enter Britain' and public opinion was very much divided. Famously, Leicester City Council took out advertisements in the African press trying to dissuade refugees from moving there. Unsurprisingly, this backfired. Much media coverage was openly racist.

The new arrivals faced a number of obstacles in addition. They had little in the way of financial resources; those leaving Uganda were only permitted to take £55. Many were therefore obliged to take menial or manual jobs at first, even if, as in many cases, they had previously been owners or managers of small businesses. Women of East African Asian origin, employed as factory workers, played a central role in the Grunwick dispute, a key episode in post-war UK industrial relations. Others managed to find sufficient capital to open small businesses, in particular corner or convenience shops. The wider environment was not favourable. In contrast to the 1950s and 1960s, the long post-war period of expansion and relative economic stability was coming to an end; unemployment was about to begin a long upward trend.

It might have been expected that being from a minority ethnic group, being an immigrant and being a refugee would be a triple disadvantage. But this has not proved to be the case. Almost half a century later, the East African Asians are generally regarded as an immigrant success story. Their educational and employment outcomes are typically as good or better than those of natives and significantly better than other immigrants of Asian origin (Anders et al., 2018). They account for a disproportionate number of immigrant-origin millionaires or successful businesspeople.

A number of explanations have been advanced for this relative success: the experience of being a refugee, resulting in personal and family resilience and an aspiration to succeed; loyalty and gratitude to the UK; the fact that, having migrated from Gujarat to Africa relatively recently, there was often recent family experience of establishing a foothold in a new society; the existence of a pre-established, albeit much smaller, Gujarati community; and the reasonably high levels of English fluency and (in some cases) education among this group.

No single explanation is likely to be adequate. The experience of more recent groups of refugees will inevitably differ across some or all of these dimensions. However, while refugee groups are of course unique in terms of where they come from, their experiences and any assets (tangible and intangible) they bring, they hold commonalities too. All have necessarily left their home country under duress, all have self-evidently made it through to a place of safety and all have experienced (at the least) very difficult transitions. So the experience of the East African Asians suggests that we should not be excessively pessimistic about the long-term prospects of refugees and their descendants. As I wrote at the height of the Syrian refugee crisis:

> Integrating refugees into our society and labour market will be, as it has been in the past, challenging. But we have done it before – with enormous benefits, both economic and social, to the UK – and there is absolutely no reason we cannot do it again.

appendix B: emigration – the impacts on countries of origin

While the focus of this book is on the impact of immigration to the UK, what about the countries from which immigrants come? If immigration is generally a benefit to the country to which an immigrant moves, then one intuitive response is that it must therefore be a cost to the country from which they move. But this is no truer than the Trumpian view that exports are good for a country's economy and that therefore imports must be bad. Neither trade nor migration are a zero-sum game. Remember, migrants – at least voluntary ones – are moving precisely because they think they can do better for themselves in another country than they can at home.

There are legitimate concerns about the impact, particularly on developing countries, if a significant proportion of the most highly skilled or highly educated segments of the population leaves – the so-called 'brain drain'. But again, teasing out the impacts is not as simple as one might think. Clearly, losing qualified doctors, particularly if they have been educated at state expense, is not likely to be good news for developing countries. But there are also countervailing impacts that may be more positive. Remittances from family members who have emigrated are a vital source of income in many countries. Emigration, sometimes combined with return migration, can over time result in networks that lead to increases in trade. Overall, the current consensus is that both can benefit – particularly if source countries and receiving countries can coordinate policies on skilled migration (Clemens et al., 2018).

An often overlooked point is that the possibility of emigration may increase the incentives for individuals to acquire skills, which can in turn benefit the domestic economy. Take the Philippines, a major source of nurses not just for the UK but also for the United States and other countries. But US policies towards the immigration of nurses have varied significantly in recent years – and research shows that the easier it was for

Filipino nurses to emigrate to the United States, the more nurses qualified in the Philippines. Indeed, the increase was more than enough to outweigh increased emigration (Abarcar and Theoharides, 2017). So the domestic health sector, if anything, benefited, when the United States adopted more liberal policies.

In some African countries, however, it does seem likely that emigration and domestic shortages of medical professionals go hand-in-hand. So while these countries only account for a small fraction of health sector migration (India and the Philippines are far bigger sources), there are negatives. But restricting immigration is not likely to help much; the reason medical professionals want to move is that pay and conditions are poor and addressing this is the main solution. Overall, the current consensus is that emigration is good for development and that more liberal migration policies in developed countries would benefit, not harm, the developing world.

There is, however, a possible exception, not in developing countries, but in the EU. This reflects demographics. Some countries, for example Latvia and Lithuania, have high levels of emigration, especially of young people, facilitated by free movement, combined with low birth rates. While emigration has fallen in the last few years, as their economies have recovered somewhat from the eurozone crisis, the risk here is a demographic downward spiral. If young (and relatively skilled) people emigrate, then the tax base is eroded. With an increasing proportion of older people, taxes will need to go up to pay for pensions and healthcare, making it even less attractive for young people to remain.

In some ways, this is similar to the problems faced by peripheral and rural areas in West European countries, where young people move to the cities, leaving behind 'hollowed-out' villages. The difference is that, within countries, the tax system can at least ensure that the young pay the pensions of the old, even if they have moved out. There are no easy answers here: even if free movement were politically reversible in the EU, restrictions on immigration elsewhere would be unlikely to help small countries in Europe to retain relatively skilled young people; they would find somewhere to go. National governments, with the help of the EU as a whole, need to find them reasons to stay. As Ireland, a small country with a history of mass emigration that has made itself attractive to both its own people and immigrants, shows, this is not impossible, but nor is it easy.

appendix C:
free movement in the eu

The EU was founded on four basic principles: free movement of labour, capital, goods and services: these 'four freedoms' were set out in the original Treaty of Rome in 1957. The point was to promote economic integration, in the widest sense, within the European area, which will now cover 27 countries (after the departure of the UK) with a population of about 500 million people.

While the primary driver may have been a desire to promote European integration for its own sake, the founders of the EU also believed that there were large economic benefits. In fact, economic theory is ambiguous on whether factor mobility (in this context, the free movement of labour and capital) is a complement or a substitute to free trade (the free movement of goods and services). That is to say, does it magnify the benefits, or is free trade on its own enough?

There is some evidence that migration promotes trade, perhaps especially trade in services, but it is far from conclusive. Whatever the strength of the economic case, other free trade areas, like the North American Free Trade Agreement, do not typically involve free movement of people. Labour mobility was seen as complementary not just to the economic aspects of European integration but, perhaps more importantly, to its wider political objectives of building a united Europe and a common European identity.

The period from the late 1950s to the early 1970s saw strong economic growth in most of the EU. However, intra-EU labour mobility remained quite low; labour demand was therefore largely met by immigration from outside the EU. The accession to the Union of Spain and Portugal in 1986 did not change this much. The 1980s and early 1990s did see a renewed push for greater market integration, launched under the umbrella of the

'Single Market'. However, the focus was very much on product markets rather than labour markets.

So, although increasingly economically integrated in terms of trade, only slightly over 1% of EU citizens lived in a country other than their country of birth by 2000. The potential downsides of this lack of mobility, despite the formal right to free movement, became more salient as the EU moved towards monetary union. In response to these concerns, the EU undertook a number of initiatives designed to turn 'free movement of workers' from a formal right to one that appeared a realistic prospect to EU citizens.

The accession in May 2004 of 10 new member states, including a number of members of the former Soviet Bloc, radically changed the dynamic of intra-EU labour mobility. It had not been seen as operating in an area where there were very large, persistent, structural differences in wage levels. Given these disparities, there was clearly a possibility of much larger intra-EU flows than had previously been the case. Indeed, the impact of accession on intra-EU migration flows was large and sustained, with substantial increases in migration to all the major economies of the existing EU, in particular the UK and Ireland. The main drivers were economic: the vast majority of migrants moved to work, attracted by either higher wages or greater job opportunities. In 2007, Bulgaria and Romania joined the EU; this too led to a significant increase in flows, although this time Spain and Italy were major destination countries.

Most recently, the eurozone crisis resulted in further changes in intra-EU migration flows. In particular, out-migration increased substantially from a number of countries where unemployment and/or youth unemployment rose sharply. Labour mobility served as an adjustment mechanism between countries that were experiencing very different economic conditions. Yet, because they were part of a single-currency area, they could not vary exchange or interest rates. In this sense, free movement worked exactly as the textbooks said it should.

Most new migrants are in employment, with employment rates for intra-EU migrants well above rates for natives in most EU countries. Given this, the overall macroeconomic impact would be expected to be positive and the evidence to date suggests it has been for most countries. Despite the considerable evidence that migration flows were driven primarily by labour market factors, there is public concern that immigrants are attracted by the prospect of generous welfare benefits and are likely to become dependent on the state. However, while there may be individuals who do indeed move between member states to take advantage of the availability of social benefits, the numbers are small and of little or no economic significance.

What about the sending countries? Out-migration has reduced unemployment and raised wages in sending countries, which also benefited from remittances. However, there are concerns about skill shortages. In Latvia and Lithuania, while emigration has clearly proved an invaluable safety valve during the crisis, there is cause for concern about the longer term demographic impact of emigration on an already ageing population with low fertility rates.

Many analysts thought that an initial surge of migrants from the new member states was likely, but that net migration was then likely to fall, as economies converged and return migration increased. However, intra-EU migration remains significant; there has clearly been a step change. So for the first time, intra-EU labour mobility is becoming as important a political and economic driver of European integration as trade and capital flows. As a result, the proportion of EU nationals living in a member state other than their birth country rose to about 3%. In a number of major countries, including Germany, the UK and Spain, it is now about 5%. In Ireland, traditionally a country of emigration rather than immigration, it is well over 1 in 10.

In contrast to immigration from outside the EU, free movement is both popular and relatively uncontroversial politically in the EU. Where there are concerns, they relate either to the use of social benefits or to 'undercutting' in the labour market, rather that free movement itself. Indeed, people exercising their free movement rights – for which they do not need visas, work permits or any other form of permission – are not necessarily seen as immigrants at all. The exception, of course, is the UK.

further reading

Anders, J., Burgess, S. and Portes, J. (2018) The Long-Term Outcomes of Refugees: Tracking the Progress of the East African Asians. IZA Discussion Paper Series. [online] Bonn: IZA Institute of Labor Economics. Available at: www.iza.org/publications/dp/11609/the-long-term-outcomes-of-refugees-tracking-the-progress-of-the-east-african-asians

Clemens, M., Huang, C., Graham, J. and Gough, K. (2018) Migration Is What You Make It: Seven Policy Decisions that Turned Challenges into Opportunities. [online] Washington, DC: Center for Global Development. Available at: www.cgdev.org/publication/migration-what-you-make-it-seven-policy-decisions-turned-challenges-opportunities

Migration Advisory Committee (2018) EAA Migration in the UK. [online] London: Migration Advisory Committee. Available at: www.gov.uk/government/publications/migration-advisory-committee-mac-report-eea-migration

Portes, J. (2015) Labour Mobility in the European Union. In *The New Palgrave Dictionary of Economics*. [online] Basingstoke: Palgrave Macmillan, pp. 1–11. Available at: www.researchgate.net/publication/311920547_Labour_Mobility_in_the_European_Union

Portes, J. (2018) New Evidence on the Economics of Immigration to the UK. [Blog] VOX CEPR Policy Portal. Available at: https://voxeu.org/article/new-evidence-economics-immigration-uk

Portes, J. (2018) The Economic Impacts of Immigration to the UK. [Blog] VOX CEPR Policy Portal. Available at: https://voxeu.org/article/economic-impacts-immigration-uk

Winder, R. (2013) *Bloody Foreigners: The Story of Immigration to Britain*. London: Little, Brown.

references

Abarcar, P. and Theoharides, C. (2017) The International Migration of Healthcare Professionals and the Supply of Educated Individuals Left Behind. In *NEUDC Conference*. [online] Available at: https://sites.tufts.edu/neudc2017/files/2017/10/paper_393.pdf

Anders, J., Burgess, S. and Portes, J. (2018) The Long-Term Outcomes of Refugees: Tracking the Progress of the East African Asians. IZA Discussion Paper Series. [online] Bonn: IZA Institute of Labor Economics. Available at: www.iza.org/publications/dp/11609/the-long-term-outcomes-of-refugees-tracking-the-progress-of-the-east-african-asians

Ballinger, S. (2018) *Many Rivers Crossed: Britain's Attitudes to Race and Integration 50 Years since 'Rivers of Blood'*. [online] London: British Future. Available at: www.britishfuture.org/wp-content/uploads/2018/04/FINAL.ManyRiversCrossed.16.4.18.pdf

Barone, G. and Mocetti, S. (2011) With a Little Help from Abroad: The Effect of Low-Skilled Immigration on the Female Labour Supply. *Labour Economics*, 18(5), 664–75.

BBC News (2015) Theresa May Pledges Asylum Reform and Immigration Crackdown. *BBC News Online*. [online] Available at: www.bbc.co.uk/news/uk-politics-34450887

Bell, B., Fasani, F. and Machin, S. (2013) Crime and Immigration: Evidence from Large Immigrant Waves. *Review of Economics and Statistics*, 95(4), 1278–90.

Campo, F., Forte, G. and Portes, J. (2018) The Impact of Migration on Productivity and Native-Born Workers' Training. Discussion Paper Series. [online] Bonn: IZA Institute of Labor Economics. Available at: http://ftp.iza.org/dp11833.pdf

Casey, L. (2016) *The Casey Review: A Review into Opportunity and Integration*. [online] London: Ministry of Housing, Communities & Local Government. Available at: https://assets.publishing.service.gov.uk/government/uploads/system/uploads/attachment_data/file/575973/The_Casey_Review_Report.pdf

Catney, G. (2013) *Has Neighbourhood Ethnic Segregation Decreased? The Dynamics of Diversity: Evidence from the 2011 Census*. [online] Manchester: Centre of Dynamics of Ethnicity (CoDE). Available at: http://hummedia.manchester.ac.uk/institutes/code/briefingsupdated/has-neighbourhood-ethnic-segregation-decreased.pdf

Clemens, M., Huang, C., Graham, J. and Gough, K. (2018) *Migration Is What You Make It: Seven Policy Decisions That Turned Challenges Into Opportunities*. [online] Washington, DC: Center for Global Development. Available at: www. cgdev.org/publication/migration-what-you-make-it-seven-policy-deci sions-turned-challenges-opportunities

Collier, P. (2013) With Britain's Population Set to Grow by 10 million... The Dangerous Liberal Myth That It's Racist to Want to Curb Immigration. *Mail Online*. [online] Available at: www.dailymail.co.uk/debate/article-2491733/ With-Britains-population-set-grow-10-million--The-dangerous-liberal-myth-racist-want-curb-immigration.html

Dustmann, C., Casanova, M., Fertig, M., Preston, I. and Schmidt, C. (2003) *The Impact of EU Enlargement on Migration Flows*. London: Home Office.

Eatwell, R. and Goodwin, M. (2018) *National Populism: The Revolt Against Liberal Democracy*. London: Pelican.

Ford, R. (2018) How Have Attitudes to Immigration Changed Since Brexit? [Blog] *Medium*. Available at: https://medium.com/@robfordmancs/how-have-attitudes-to-immigration-changed-since-brexit-e37881f55530

Geay, C., McNally, S. and Telhaj, S. (2013) Non-Native Speakers of English in the Classroom: What Are the Effects on Pupil Performance? *Economic Journal*, *123*(570), F281–307.

Giulietti, C. (2014) The Welfare Magnet Hypothesis and the Welfare Take-Up of Migrants. *IZA World of Labor*. [online] Available at: https://wol.iza.org/uploads/ articles/37/pdfs/welfare-magnet-hypothesis-and-welfare-take-up-of-migrants. pdf

Giulietti, C. and Yan, Z. (2018) *The Impact of Immigration on the Well-being of UK Natives*. [online] London: Migration Advisory Committee. Available at: https:// assets.publishing.service.gov.uk/government/uploads/system/uploads/attach ment_data/file/740985/Giulietti__2018_.pdf

Giuntella, O., Nicodemo, C. and Vargas-Silva, C. (2018) The Effects of Immigration on NHS Waiting Times. *Journal of Health Economics*, *58*, 123–43.

Glover, S., Gott, C., Loizillon, A., Portes, J., Price, R., Spencer, S., Srinivasan, V. and Willis, C. (2001) *Migration: An Economic and Social Analysis*. London: Home Office.

Goodwin, M. and Milazzo, C. (2017) Taking Back Control? Investigating the Role of Immigration in the 2016 Vote for Brexit. *British Journal of Politics and International Relations*, *19*(3), 450–64. [online] Available at: https://journals.sagepub.com/doi/ abs/10.1177/1369148117710799

Gordon, I., Scanlon, K., Travers, T. and Whitehead, C. (2009) *Economic Impact on the London and UK Economy of an Earned Regularisation of Irregular Migrants to the UK*. London: Mayor of London.

Hill, C. (1997) *Puritanism and Revolution*. New York: St. Martin's Press.

Home Office (2018) *The UK's Future Skills-Based Immigration System*. [online] London: Home Office. Available at: https://www.gov.uk/government/publica tions/the-uks-future-skills-based-immigration-system

Independent (2015) *Theresa May's Speech to the Conservative Party Conference – in full. Independent.* [online] Available at: www.independent.co.uk/news/uk/politics/theresa-may-s-speech-to-the-conservative-party-conference-in-full-a6681901.html

Ipsos MORI (2018) *A Review of Survey Research on Muslims in Britain.* [online] London: Ipsos MORI: Social Research Institute. Available at: www.ipsos.com/sites/default/files/ct/publication/documents/2018-03/a-review-of-survey-research-on-muslims-in-great-britain-ipsos-mori_0.pdf

Jaumotte, F., Koloskova, K. and Saxena, S. (2016) *Impact of Migration on Income Levels in Advanced Economies.* Washington, DC: International Monetary Fund.

Jivraj, S. (2012) *How Has Ethnic Diversity Grown 1991–2001–2011? The Dynamics of Diversity: Evidence from the 2011 Census.* [online] Manchester: Centre on Dynamics of Ethnicity (CoDE). Available at: http://hummedia.manchester.ac.uk/institutes/code/briefings/dynamicsofdiversity/how-has-ethnic-diversity-grown-1991-2001-2011.pdf

Kaufmann, E. (2018) *Whiteshift.* London: Allen Lane (Penguin).

Kelley, N., Khan, D. and Sharrock, S. (2017) *Racial Prejudice in Britain Today.* [online] London: NatCen Social Research. Available at: http://natcen.ac.uk/media/1488132/racial-prejudice-report_v4.pdf

Migration Advisory Committee (2018) *Migration Advisory Committee (MAC) Report: EEA Migration.* [online] London: Migration Advisory Committee. Available at: www.gov.uk/government/publications/migration-advisory-committee-mac-report-eea-migration

Mukherjee, S. (2019) *Our Migration Story: The Making of Britain.* [online] Ourmigrationstory.org.uk. Available at: www.ourmigrationstory.org.uk/oms/dad-abhai-naoroji-mp-for-central-finsbury-1892-1895

Murray, D. (2017) *The Strange Death of Europe: Immigration, Identity, Islam.* London: Bloomsbury Continuum.

Nathan, M. (2014) The Wider Economic Impacts of High-Skilled Migrants: A Survey of the Literature for Receiving Countries. *IZA Journal of Migration,* 3(4), 1–20.

Nickell, S. and Saleheen, J. (2015) *The Impact of Immigration on Occupational Wages: Evidence from Britain.* [online] London: Bank of England. Available at: www.bankofengland.co.uk/working-paper/2015/the-impact-of-immigration-on-occupational-wages-evidence-from-britain

Nowrasteh, A. (2018) The White House's Misleading & Error Ridden Narrative on Immigrants and Crime. [Blog] Washington, DC: Cato Institute. Available at: www.cato.org/blog/white-houses-misleading-error-ridden-narrative-immigrants-crime

Office of National Statistics (2016) [online] Ons.gov.uk. Available at: www.ons.gov.uk/file?uri=/peoplepopulationandcommunity/populationandmigration/internationalmigration/bulletins/migrationstatisticsquarterlyreport/may2016/55416447.png

Ons.gov.uk (n.d.) [online] Available at: www.ons.gov.uk/chartimage?uri=/peoplepopulationandcommunity/populationandmigration/internationalmigration/bulletins/ukpopulationbycountryofbirthandnationality/2017/d6d98cc8

Oxford Economics (2018) *The Fiscal Impact of Immigration on the UK: A Report for the Migration Advisory Committee*. [online] London: Migration Advisory Committee. Available at: www.oxfordeconomics.com/recent-releases/8747673d-3b26-439b-9693-0e250df6dbba

Phillips, T. (2005) Sleepwalking to Segregation. *The Times*. [online] Available at: www.thetimes.co.uk/article/sleepwalking-to-segregation-jhz9ktlwlzg

Platt, L. (2009) *Ethnicity and Family: Relationships Within and Between Ethnic Groups: An Analysis Using The Labour Force Survey*. EHRC unnumbered research reports. [online] Manchester: Equality and Human Rights Commission. Available at: http://eprints.lse.ac.uk/55561/

Press Association (2012) Ethnic Minorities in UK Feel Most British, Research Finds. *Guardian*. [online] Available at: www.theguardian.com/uk/2012/jun/30/ethnic-minorities-uk-british-research

Rodrik, D. (2016) *The Surprising Thing About the Backlash Against Globalization*. [online] Geneva: World Economic Forum. Available at: www.weforum.org/agenda/2016/07/the-surprising-thing-about-the-backlash-against-globalization

Thatcher, M. (1978) TV Interview for *Granada World in Action*. Available at: www.margaretthatcher.org/document/103485.

Warsi, S. (2012) Ugandan Asians Are Part of Britain's Secret Weapon for Success. *Spectator*. [online] Available at: https://blogs.spectator.co.uk/2012/12/ugandan-asians-are-part-of-britains-secret-weapon-for-success/

index